Seeking Your Better Self

Timely Virtues for a Turbulent World

Jeffrey Nesteruk

Pennsylvania, United States

Copyright © 2026 by John Wiley & Sons, Inc.

All rights reserved, including rights for text and data mining and training of artificial intelligence technologies or similar technologies.

Published by John Wiley & Sons, Inc., Hoboken, New Jersey.

No part of this publication may be reproduced, stored in a retrieval system, or transmitted in any form or by any means, electronic, mechanical, photocopying, recording, scanning, or otherwise, except as permitted under Section 107 or 108 of the 1976 United States Copyright Act, without either the prior written permission of the Publisher, or authorization through payment of the appropriate per-copy fee to the Copyright Clearance Center, Inc., 222 Rosewood Drive, Danvers, MA 01923, (978) 750-8400, fax (978) 750-4470, or on the web at www.copyright.com. Requests to the Publisher for permission should be addressed to the Permissions Department, John Wiley & Sons, Inc., 111 River Street, Hoboken, NJ 07030, (201) 748-6011, fax (201) 748-6008, or online at http://www.wiley.com/go/permission.

The manufacturer's authorized representative according to the EU General Product Safety Regulation is Wiley-VCH GmbH, Boschstr. 12, 69469 Weinheim, Germany, e-mail: Product_Safety@wiley.com.

Trademarks: Wiley and the Wiley logo are trademarks or registered trademarks of John Wiley & Sons, Inc. and/or its affiliates in the United States and other countries and may not be used without written permission. All other trademarks are the property of their respective owners. John Wiley & Sons, Inc. is not associated with any product or vendor mentioned in this book.

Limit of Liability/Disclaimer of Warranty: The contents of this work are intended to further general scientific research, understanding, and discussion only and are not intended and should not be relied upon as recommending or promoting scientific method, diagnosis, or treatment by physicians for any particular patient. In view of ongoing research, equipment modifications, changes in governmental regulations, and the constant flow of information relating to the use of medicines, equipment, and devices, the reader is urged to review and evaluate the information provided in the package insert or instructions for each medicine, equipment, or device for, among other things, any changes in the instructions or indication of usage and for added warnings and precautions. While the publisher and the authors have used their best efforts in preparing this work, including a review of the content of the work, neither the publisher nor the authors make any representations or warranties with respect to the accuracy or completeness of the contents of this work and specifically disclaim all warranties, including without limitation any implied warranties of merchantability or fitness for a particular purpose. No warranty may be created or extended by sales representatives, written sales materials or promotional statements for this work. The fact that an organization, website, or product is referred to in this work as a citation and/or potential source of further information does not mean that the publisher and authors endorse the information or services the organization, website, or product may provide or recommendations it may make. This work is sold with the understanding that the publisher is not engaged in rendering professional services. The advice and strategies contained herein may not be suitable for your situation. You should consult with a specialist where appropriate. Further, readers should be aware that websites listed in this work may have changed or disappeared between when this work was written and when it is read. Neither the publisher nor authors shall be liable for any loss of profit or any other commercial damages, including but not limited to special, incidental, consequential, or other damages.

For general information on our other products and services or for technical support, please contact our Customer Care Department within the United States at (800) 762-2974, outside the United States at (317) 572-3993 or fax (317) 572-4002.

Wiley also publishes its books in a variety of electronic formats. Some content that appears in print may not be available in electronic formats. For more information about Wiley products, visit our web site at www.wiley.com.

Library of Congress Cataloging-in-Publication Data has been applied for:

Paper Back ISBN: 9781394328734
ePub ISBN: 9781394328741
ePDF ISBN: 9781394328758

Cover Design: Wiley
Cover Image: © Eastlyn Bright/stock.adobe.com

To my wife, Hedi, and my daughter, Caroline, who together light up my world.

Contents

Acknowledgments *vii*

1 **Introduction** *1*
An Invitation to Ethical Reflection

2 **Our Relationship with Ourselves** *16*
A Holistic Mind

3 **Our Relationship with Others** *45*
An Empathetic Heart

4 **Our Relationship with Things** *74*
An Attentive Eye

5 **Our Relationship with That Which Is Greater Than Ourselves** *102*
An Open Spirit

6 **Conclusion – And Now What?** *132*
Telling Your Own Story

Notes *143*
Bibliography *144*
Review Heading Index *148*

Acknowledgments

I wish to thank the following individuals who through their professional expertise, personal friendship, or perceptive insights have enabled me to write this book: Claire Preisser, John Garic, Rebecca Crews, Timothy Sipe, Robert Gethner, Kerry Whiteside, John Giglio, Gabriel Finder, Janine Fiedler, Thomas Karel, Erik Anderson, Laura Pople, Janaki Kumudam Gothandaraman, William Sullivan.

1

Introduction

An Invitation to Ethical Reflection

> *"There is only one journey. Going inside yourself."*
>
> Rainer Maria Rilke

Doing an Inward Turn

Wobbly Moments

Writing this book is rooted in my own wobbly moments. I'm sure you've had your share of wobbly moments too. We all do.

At their core, wobbly moments are those unsettling experiences in your life when you're not sure how to react or go forward. It could be a personal relationship that veered into unexpected or painful territory, leaving you struggling to regain your emotional balance. It could be the professional ladder you've been assiduously climbing was knocked out from under you, its base unexpectedly upended by a change in management or a shift in office politics. Uncomfortable as they can be, there is a value in recognizing and embracing your wobbly moments.

Like most college teachers, I am at ease in my chosen field. Having studied literature, philosophy, and law, I have made my academic reputation as a specialist in ethics, exploring the moral dilemmas of the contemporary workplace. But with this achievement has come my own wobbly moments, arising from a disconcerting sense of how I am often unable to talk about what I see as most significant in our moral lives within the technical debates and language of my discipline. Too many times something essential surfaces for me only after class, as when a theory readily espoused in my lecture does little to assuage a conflict I'm having with a colleague or when I am fumbling for words as a struggling student relates a painful experience in the privacy of my office.

Seeking your Better Self: Timely Virtues for a Turbulent World, First Edition. Jeffrey Nesteruk.
© 2026 John Wiley & Sons, Inc. All rights reserved, including rights for text and data mining and training of artificial intelligence technologies or similar technologies. Published 2026 by John Wiley & Sons, Inc.

The Story I Want to Tell

The series of reflections contained in *Seeking Your Better Self* fills this gap. Hoping to engage you to take a deeper look at your own life, I focus here on everyday topics – subjects such as money, conversation, stress, and forgiveness – but do so in a way that reveals their deeper significance. Specifically, I bring into view how exploring such topics can illuminate our strivings and aspirations, our struggle, as I like to put it, to be our better selves. As we go forward, you should expect as many questions as answers.

In writing this book, I grapple with these topics through the puzzles and choices of my own life. In doing so, I reveal a fuller version of myself than my students normally see – the less secure, more fallible me that exists outside the classroom. My hope is that by providing this more intimate portrait, I can encourage a reciprocity of spirit among all those who read this book to do likewise. Following each topical reflection, there are helpful prompts designed to engage you in exploring and extending each reflection's insights. I encourage you to tap into your own wobbly moments and in this way bring the book's insights into your own life. My hope is that you, like me, are willing to acknowledge your own unfinished character and thus are ready to accept my invitation to participate in an undertaking aimed at your own moral exploration and growth. This approach aspires to make visible the personal moral engagement often missing from more academic discussions of ethics. It can reveal the stories behind the arguments.

The story I have to tell is a personal one. It's about morality, yet it is never moralistic. The topical reflections here are more associational than argumentative, designed to provide a glimpse of what is admirable and worth striving for in our day-to-day routines. By exposing the many possibilities for integrity, dignity, and well-being in ordinary life, I hope to provoke us all to think more about what it means to live well.

The undertaking of the book involves an expanding enactment of what psychologists call metacognition – an "awareness and understanding of one's own thought processes," as one online dictionary defines it. Each new awareness or level of understanding alters your thinking, just as every choice you make helps to define the person you are becoming. The hoped-for movement is from yourself to other persons to things in your world to your larger aspirations.

It is thus a movement from the problems *in* your life to the purpose *of* your life. *Seeking Your Better Self* is designed to encourage you to adopt an evaluative stance, engaging its ideas and exercises, its aspirations and inquiries, with a critical eye. It seeks to open up questions in and for your life to see where you might take them. Along the way, I will be telling my story with the hope of you reflecting on and telling your own.

Ethics as Relationships

The structure of *Seeking Your Better Self* arises out of the basic nature of ethics. Most fundamentally, ethics is about relationships. Renewing our moral lives thus involves gaining a deeper understanding of these relationships and acquiring the skills and insights necessary for enriching them. In so doing, we can bring a vitality to our lives our material achievements cannot provide. For living morally is the key to living meaningfully.

To see the connection of relationships to ethics, try imagining an individual human being without any relationships. You might think, for instance, of a person stranded for the rest of his life on a remote, uninhabited island. Alone and cut off from any contact with the rest of human society, this modern-day Robinson Crusoe would have a very different moral life from the kind we typically experience in our more complex, contemporary lives. He would not, for example, experience the ethical dilemma so many of us struggle with of properly balancing family and career. He wouldn't experience such a dilemma because his life is devoid of the relationships that give rise to it. He has no boss at work demanding he stay late. He has no daughter at home waiting to be taken to her first Little League game.

Indeed, this isolated individual would have little need for many of the ethical values we typically require to get through the day. For, on the surface at least, his conduct wouldn't affect anyone else. He could say and do what he wants without consequence to his fellow human beings. Whether he spent his days writing a brilliant novel or drinking himself into a stupor would be, at one level at least, all morally the same. For any novel he writes will never be read, any hangover he suffers won't make him late for work.

Revealed in this simple mental exercise is the particular connection between relationships and ethics. The ethical dilemmas of our lives arise from the very relationships that give our lives richness and value. Remove a set of relationships from a person's existence – as we did with our island castaway – and we change the nature of that person's moral life, often drastically. Absent human companionship, our island prisoner experiences a dramatically diminished moral life in which so many of his choices no longer matter in a way they once did. But as his choices diminish in moral significance, so do his opportunities for a satisfying and meaningful life. Fantasies of self-indulgence aside, few of us would choose the life he now must face.

The Four Fundamental Relationships

Broadly speaking, there are four kinds of relationships with which our moral lives are inevitably intertwined. They are (1) the relationship we have with ourselves,

(2) the relationship we have with others, (3) the relationship we have with things, and (4) the relationship we have with that which is greater than ourselves – the spiritual character of life. Leading a more meaningful life entails attending more deeply to each of these relationships.

We have a relationship with ourselves because of our distinctively human capacity for self-reflection. As individuals, we have the ability to take a step back from ourselves and evaluate what we see. Our relationship with ourselves is the relationship between the self that's seeing and the self that's being seen. While this division within ourselves provides the potential for moral growth, it also presents a formidable moral challenge. The challenge here is one of developing character, becoming whole, and achieving integrity.

Along with our relationship with ourselves is our relationship with others – the kind of relationship we took from our hypothetical island castaway. When speaking of ethics, we regularly mention our relationships with others, and these relationships are clearly crucial. Yet typically we miss a significant moral dimension of such relationships. In an important sense, we create and develop ourselves through our relationships with others. Thus, a central challenge here is creating ennobling relationships, ones that, in a moral sense, make us better while we are bettering the lives of others.

There is also our relationship with things. Because they are such an intimate part of our daily routines, the things of the world – the places we inhabit, the possessions we work for, and the practices we engage in – have a greater moral significance than we generally acknowledge. As of late, this has become especially true of the increasingly pervasive technologies in our lives, from TikTok to the Metaverse to ChatGPT. Though they may appear neutral in this regard, each thing in the world has a moral tilt to it. Involving ourselves with it pushes us one way or another. The moral danger of our practical engagements – think, for instance, of an inordinate desire for money – is that they can subtly distort our values or influence our choices.

Finally, there is the relationship we have with that which is greater than ourselves – the spiritual character of life. This more expansive horizon or context is, of course, subject to a variety of interpretations. But in the end, renewing our relationships here grounds the renewal of all our other relationships. When we enter the transcendental domain of our lives, we often experience something essential yet mysterious, unavoidable yet difficult to explain. Indeed, the frequent mark of authentic spiritual experience is the struggle that ensues when we attempt to put it into words. The moral struggle here is giving voice to what we can't perfectly express, accepting how life is always larger than our conceptions of it.

Deeply attuned to the fundamental relationships that enrich our lives, *Seeking Your Better Self* aims for ethics in a positive, welcoming voice. It is an aspirational guide marked by humility and hope. It is for individuals who wish to understand how embedding goals such as financial security, professional achievement, or public recognition in rich moral relationships can best contribute to lives worth living. For everyone who wishes to define their own version of the good life, *Seeking Your Better Self* does more than showcase what is inspirational in our lives. It helps us to ask and understand why.

Raising Your Moral Sights

I often tell my students that I am in the human potential business. I do so because the key to getting the most out of our class time together is to obtain their commitment to raise their sights. They need to be open to the possibility that they are more than they currently think they are – better than they yet imagine.

In our common time together now, I will likewise be asking you to raise your sights, to consider the possibility that the moral potential in your life is greater than you currently realize.

The relationship-based conception of ethics provides you with the structure for your undertaking of moral exploration and growth by offering a chapter dedicated to each of the four fundamental relationships at the core of ethics. Each chapter begins by highlighting an aspiring attribute of character, the central virtue that exemplifies the ethical possibilities implicit in a specific relationship. This virtue captures the moral excellence present in the highest development of that relationship. Thus, the chapter on our relationship with others focuses on the virtue of an empathetic heart. This virtue embodies a personal aspiration to foster an imaginative and sympathetic understanding of the experiences of others.

Coupled with the description of the central virtue at stake is an overview of the relationship, outlining its core ethical challenges and opportunities. Thus, the chapter on the relationship with ourselves, for example, addresses the challenges posed by the multiple tensions each of us experiences within ourselves and the opportunities offered for creating a more coherent self, one capable and more adept at integrating the values we espouse with the lives we actually lead.

In this way, each chapter sets the stage for reflections on individual topics that follow, with each reflection focusing on an everyday occurrence or encounter that involves the basic moral relationship at stake. Arranged so as to stimulate a deeper examination of this basic moral relationship, these topical pieces expose the potential for a larger awareness of the moral meanings of everyday life. Thus, for example, the chapter on our relationship with things sets the stage for topical reflections, finding moral meanings in everything from our struggle to manage life's "details" to everyday stresses over "moving" to the awkwardness of dealing with a "chatbot" over the phone when you dearly wish to speak to a fellow human being.

Raising your moral sights brings into view telling reminders of how asking more of ourselves can lead to more meaningful lives. It can aid you in discovering the unexpected sublimity in ordinary moments. It can offer you a renewed appreciation for savoring common, human encounters.

Most of all, it will let you in on a secret hidden in plain sight: there's an ethical abundance to everyday life.

Beginning Where You Are

One thing I've learned about teaching over the years is that good teachers always begin wherever students are, but good teachers never leave students where they are. As I sometimes tell my students, "I want to give you a hard time – lovingly!"

Thus, the process I'm inviting you into here is a transformational one, starting at whatever point in your life you happen to be, but then encouraging you forward. It's my way of giving you a hard time – lovingly!

Such a process incorporates four key features:

Accessible: Unlike books that are heavily focused on theory or couched in the technical language of disciplinary specialists, this book is oriented toward engaging a broader, more diverse audience of readers. All it asks of you is that you are ethically curious.

Motivational: By grounding its model for ethics in the healthy and satisfying relationships we all desire, *Seeking Your Better Self* provides a motivational impetus for personal development. It is designed not only to help you clarify your own version of a good life but also to foster in you a stronger and more robust desire to achieve it.

Relatable: As a variety of short, topical reflections from daily life accompany this model, the book presents its insights in an easily relatable form.

Action-oriented: With stimulating prompts after each reflection aimed at helping you bring the reflection's insights into your own life, *Seeking Your Better Self* is for those who are ready to challenge themselves.

As an ethics book that is accessible, motivational, relatable, and action-oriented, it is for individuals who are amid their own wobbly moments, asking in one way or another, "And now what?"

Bringing Your Whole Self

For much of our formal education, we are oriented toward performing rather than learning. Our school systems demand it – and our own insecurities too often compel it. I have often felt in my teaching career that many students only share their most superficial selves. It is always a gratifying moment when their more capacious selves – their stumbling alongside their soaring selves – break through. For education to work, you have to bring your whole self to the endeavor.

By drawing upon the relationship-based conception of ethics in *Seeking Your Better Self*, I hope to engage your whole self. By grounding its model for ethics in the healthy and satisfying relationships that we all want, this book's conception of ethics aims for an integration of two senses of our aspirations for a "good life" – "good" in the sense of "admirable" and "good" in the sense of "desired." In focusing on your whole self, *Seeking Your Better Self* thus envisions the potential for a virtuous life that is also one marked by happiness and personal fulfillment.

Of course, there are many times when what is ethically admirable diverges from what we might more immediately desire. Any tired parent of a newborn desperate for a few hours of sleep who hears his child crying at 2 a.m. knows what I mean!

But that's hardly the whole picture. We can have worthy desires, and they are something worth striving for. I recall when I was first married, I looked out of our window one morning and saw my wife pulling into our driveway just as a rainy downpour began. While I would normally prefer staying dry and warm inside, I ran out without thinking to give her an umbrella and help her into our home.

It's not that my rushing outside was any great moral achievement. I suspect it's something that most of us would probably do. But what was striking to me upon reflection about the experience is that I didn't for a moment feel in any way deprived or that my action involved a sacrifice of any sort. Something good – an admirable concern to help my wife – was something that, at the moment, I in fact desired.

So, bringing your whole self to your endeavor here entails being open to developing worthy desires. A flourishing life – a fully satisfying life – is one in which what is praiseworthy, what is worth striving for, is equally one that is pleasurable and ultimately gratifying.

Tapping the Life-enhancing Power of Reflection

Our Out-of-kilter Lives

A while back, I was talking with an old friend, and he suddenly stopped in the middle of the conversation and said, "Jeff, you're so reflective, I feel like I'm talking to a mirror." He chuckled a bit, and I did too at his good-natured jesting.

No doubt I have a reflective bent. At the end of the day, I can happily sit on our outdoor patio looking over the trees and letting my thoughts wander. With some frequency, my wife has had to remind me that I've forgotten to wash the dishes.

I'm sure it hasn't helped that my academic pursuits have spanned literature, philosophy, and law, all fields that prompt one to take a deeper look at things.

They all invite a curiosity that is restless with the surface of things, skeptical of received wisdom that hasn't been personally affirmed.

But I'm often struck by how my inclination toward reflection puts me out of sync with much of the hectic bustle of our contemporary world. I see it in the harried lines at the supermarket and the rush for seats on the commuter train. I hear about it when my wife tells me the fellow driving behind her gave her the finger for obeying the speed limit. Even the gentle kidding of my old friend was a subtle reminder of how my disposition was far from widely shared.

Perhaps surprisingly, I notice it even in my interaction with many of my students, bright young people on the cusp of adulthood enjoying the leisure and rich stimulating environment of a good liberal arts college. In the past, during a break in my seminars, students would eagerly wish to continue the conversation, challenging each other or coming up to me to share an idea or pose a question. Now, during the breaks, the phones quickly come out and there is mostly silence, broken only by the tapping of emails or the beeps of text updates.

We often hear how we live in a distracted age, overloaded with information and ill-equipped to process it. The pace of our daily lives can leave us feeling out-of-kilter, struggling to keep our balance. Life for many of us has a pressured, jittery feel. We're left with an ill-defined, yet abiding sense that something is just not right.

Such a distracted age is itself a poignant call for a deeper, more authentic reflection in our lives. But it is a call that we regularly leave unheeded.

Keeping Reflection at Bay

Why do we often keep reflection at bay? There are many levels to our resistance here, some immediate and on the surface, some deeper and more profound. Many of which I've struggled with at one point or another in my life.

Most immediately, there is the pressing stuff of daily life. Navigating the automated telephone maze to make a doctor's appointment. The report you promised your boss this week. The frozen website portal you're trying to use for recalibrating your retirement investments. While the specifics may vary, we all feel these run-of-the-mill pressures, regardless of status or stage of life. They pop up regularly as alerts on your phone even as you open your eyes and then subtly stalk you throughout the day.

While the insistent demands of constant connection can be unpleasant, our information overload with its unending stimulation also has an addictive quality. With ready access to so much information, we often experience a growing sense of FOMO or, as they say, fear of missing out. As a young boy prior to cell phones, if my mother was late in picking me up from football practice, I often had nothing more interesting to do than stare at my shoes. Now, when I'm waiting in the parking lot to pick up my daughter, I'm checking the latest on Google News while I text a colleague at work. After a while, if you're always "On," it's easy to forget what "Off" feels like.

Amid all the other obligations and opportunities of an active life, you might ask of a deeper commitment to reflection, "Is it worth the bother?" In a fast-paced, get-ahead world, it can appear to be a time-squandering trap for being left behind. It's easy to bring to mind more immediately useful ways of spending your time. I remember my grandmother could never completely accept my seemingly unproductive routine of jogging. "If you've got so much energy," she'd be saying, "Go mow the lawn!"

For many high-achieving professionals today, "busy" also has an especially seductive appeal for shoring up their sense of self-worth. It is certainly an appeal to which I am not immune. But I wonder if this skepticism about the value of pausing to reflect masks an unease about the consequences of leading a more reflective life.

This frenetic pace of life can frequently be intertwined with a deeper and more subtle form of self deception. I remember sharing a drive home with a talented friend of mine, an Ivy League graduate who complained of a deep dissatisfaction with his job. Knowing his capabilities and the opportunities potentially available to him, I asked had he thought about leaving. With a dismissive look at me for having raised the question, he said, "I don't even have the time to think about it." I could see the conversation wasn't going any further, as he turned his eyes back to the road.

In his response, I was uncomfortably reminded of myself at earlier points in my life. Deeper, more authentic reflection has the potential to be life-probing and life-altering. It's a psychological version of skating on thin ice, not knowing in advance where the cracks might be or the depths to which you might suddenly plunge. We all have our tacit fears and unarticulated anxieties. There's an understandable wariness about what reflection might reveal about your life, what it might force you to confront or change.

The Hard Work of Reflection

And yet, even if you're inclined toward reflection, I think the kind of reflection we're after here is hard to do well. Why?

At root, the problem is so many of us have not had the opportunity to develop the dispositions and acquire the skills needed to do this deeper reflection well. Genuine reflection, in many ways, is so far from our prevalent experiences today that we may fail to recognize our deficiencies in this regard. But developing the capabilities to do reflection well is essential in any sustained undertaking of moral exploration and growth. Thus, a core aspiration of *Seeking Your Better Self* is providing the framework and strategies that enable you to engage in deeper, more authentic reflection.

This more robust reflection I hope to bring to life here is far from anxious fretting, compulsive thinking, or considering something only long enough to provide a justification for a preconceived belief. Such disabling forms of our mental life are already far too prevalent.

The reflection I wish to bring into view here is instead a deeper, more philosophical form of reflection, a *virtue-infused* reflection. In its most developed form, a virtue-infused reflection engages the feeling of wonder, the practice of questions, the perception of insights, and ultimately the transformation of self. It is a continual exercise in self-renewal. You ineluctably become a different person as the process unfolds. It is in these transformative possibilities that the distinctive nature of ethical reflection comes to the fore.

As a virtue-infused reflection, it involves a lifelong commitment to an always unperfected practice. As is true of achieving excellence in many of life's endeavors, from finishing a marathon to flourishing in a marriage, it takes dedication – and time. Time for initial choices to develop into persistent habits that evolve into an enduring character.

An essential feature of the process of learning how to do this ethical reflection is the way it dissolves many of the obstacles we identified that inhibit a more examined life. The process will help loosen the grip of the pressure of your daily to-do lists, free you from the addictive dynamics of information overload, and uncover the subtle forms of self-deception that impede the development of your better self.

This book will thus work best not as a "fast read," but rather as a "slow read" with much for you to ponder along the way. For it to work, you need to give it the time that you and the endeavor deserve.

Facebook's "Move Fast and Break Things" may have served it well at first. But as a larger life philosophy, it has its limits. If all we can do is move quickly, we might find that the unacknowledged consequence of Facebook's early dictum is that the things we break are the most valuable parts of ourselves.

Starting with the Virtues

A Preview of the Four Virtues

Virtue-infused reflection is not mere calculation or a form of strategic problem-solving. This is because it is not simply about what you will do but, more fundamentally, about who you are. Thus, this deeper, more philosophical reflection must tap into your underlying values and draw upon your ethical core.

As it draws upon your basic ethical identity, this distinctive form of reflection entails developing the four virtues that are the mark of excellence in the four relationships at the core of ethics. It is these four virtues that ground and guide the reflection we are after.

In capsule form, the four virtues are:

1. A Holistic Mind: Reflection here aims for a clarity of thinking that fosters a coherent self. When your aims are scattered, when the pushes and pulls of your life are in tension, and when the varied pieces of yourself don't fit together, you lack the personal integrity that the practice of reflection requires.
2. An Empathetic Heart: Reflection here requires a deepening of emotion that enables an imaginative and sympathetic understanding of the experience of others. For only a blinkered version of reflection is possible within a self-centered framework. Without an emotional awareness that others have as rich of an interior life as you do, reflection can never reach its higher aspirations.
3. An Attentive Eye: Reflection here aims at an expansion of perception to cultivate a greater awareness of things in your world. For reflection to probe beneath the surface, it must have a developed appreciation of the difference such a rich intellectual and sensory perception of your environment can make.
4. An Open Spirit: Reflection here adopts a skepticism of received wisdom that hasn't been personally affirmed. It thus must nurture an open disposition. It allows doubts alongside beliefs and questions accompanying answers in the process of discerning one's purpose. Alive to the ever-present possibility of change, it entails an intrinsic affirmation of hope.

As thus understood, virtue-infused reflection aspires to a clarity of thought, a deepening of emotion, an expansion of perception, and an affirmation of hope. Let's look at each in turn.

Clarity of Thought

Clarity of thought is hard for all of us. Yet paradoxically, it is something that we often take for granted in ourselves.

Like many professors, I see this most immediately in my students' writing. This is because of the way their writing concretizes their thoughts, giving them a more definite or specific shape. In doing so, it readily brings to the fore any lack of clarity in their expression.

In going over a student's answer from an in-class essay exam, I often have students read their answers out loud to me. Often, something they thought they had written simply wasn't there or was only there in a confused form. This occurs because in the act of writing, students were aware of both their own hazy stream of consciousness at that moment and what they actually committed to the page. But when they later read out loud their essay, all they see is what they have explicitly articulated in their exam book, something that frequently falls short of saying clearly everything they meant to express.

So much of teaching involves bringing to students' awareness unrealized contradictions in their own thinking. It certainly can make them uncomfortable and thus needs to be done carefully and with an appropriate sensitivity. As Leon Festinger noted, cognitive dissidence – when your beliefs or behaviors exhibit inconsistency – is a psychologically uncomfortable state for us. But its hidden virtue is that this very uncomfortableness serves as a spur to clarify our thinking and thus offers the opportunity to see things anew.

In aspiring to think more clearly, we face our share of psychological challenges, first and foremost, the well-documented phenomenon of "self-serving bias." As David G. Myers puts it, "We perceive ourselves as better than most and explain events in self-enhancing ways." One finding that particularly struck home for me revealed that more than 90% of college professors believed their teaching was better than average. This study brought about more personal wobbly moments than I care to admit, as I would regularly second-guess myself after thinking a class went well.

Beyond the pervasiveness of self-serving bias, there is the challenge posed by "motivated reasoning." This psychological dynamic causes us to reason about something only long enough to have a ready justification for what we already believed prior to doing any reflection. We don't proceed to the next step to challenge this preconceived belief. So, the ever-present danger is cutting short an ongoing process.

We are complicated creatures. Walt Whitman famously said, "I contain multitudes." That is both a marvelous thing – we are richer than we imagine – and something that should inspire us to clarify our thinking in reflecting more fully and carefully.

Deepening of Emotion

While it's common to think of reflection as simply an intellectual activity, this significantly diminishes reflection's power. We can learn as much from our feelings – indeed, often more – as we learn from our thinking. In fact, our feelings often, in a tacit or inchoate way, hint at things that we are not yet ready to put in a discursive fashion. Emotions are the thoughts we can't yet express.

Jonathan Haidt offers a wonderful visual metaphor here. It is that of the tiny Rider upon an enormous Elephant. The Rider represents the rational, analytical side of ourselves and the Elephant captures the emotional, impulsive side of ourselves. While the smaller Rider may hold the reins and see where he wants to go, it is the irrational yet much larger Elephant who provides the motivation and thus ultimately bears most heavily upon our choices and direction.

Thus, it is important for full-fledged reflection, not only to think things through but to *feel* things through. Feeling things through often involves bracketing your intellectual side, holding your thinking at bay. With our motivating reasoning and other psychological defenses, we frequently attempt to literally *rationalize* things. That is, we attempt to understand in rational terms, aspects of our interior experience that are far from rational. It doesn't mean such experiences lack a logic of their own. It simply means they make sense in ways other than the linear way our rational side prefers.

Benjamin Franklin was wise to urge a bit of caution in relying solely on our rational capacities in reflecting upon our lives. "So convenient a thing it is to be a *rational* creature," he said with his characteristic wit, "since it enables one to find or make a reason for everything one has a mind to do." We all fall prey to this at one time or another.

While achieving clarity of thought involves disciplining our thoughts – trying to get the small Rider to hold the reins more tightly – feeling things through can involve letting our thoughts wander, not subjecting them to any conscious control, something we'll explore in coming chapters.

But for now, I simply wish to note that if reflection is to be fully life-enhancing, our thinking needs our emotions as an ever-present participant in the process, sometimes willing to defer, but never shy and always available. Only then can we learn to ride the Elephant well.

Expansion of Perception

Often overlooked in acquiring the skills and habits for deeper, more life-enhancing reflection is the environment in which you are mulling things over. The unfolding character of your reflection involves more than a detached thinking and feeling things through, even when you are alone. It is intimately bound up in your perceptions, your intellectual and sensory experience of the settings in which you find yourself.

There's a reason for everything from religious cathedrals to beautiful college campuses to the quiet, secluded paths of public parks. The cathedrals inspire awe in their congregations, the aesthetic appeal of campuses encourages the educational aspirations of students, and quiet, secluded paths sooth and calm us in our walks. While reflection often requires keeping the hustle and bustle of daily life momentarily at bay, whatever new environment you enter into for your quiet moments is more than an escape. It has a potentially positive contribution to make through the ways it expands your perceptions as you take in its subtleties and uncover its layered meanings.

Angela Duckworth and her colleagues have stressed the importance of "situational self-control strategies" as a way of avoiding temptations, such as an overindulgence in junk foods. It helps not to have unhealthy foods within arm's reach in your kitchen. With our many excellent local ice cream shops, I love going out for ice cream. (Truth be told, I enjoy ice cream just about any time or place.) But one advantage to having to go out for these creamy treats, rather than simply grabbing them from my refrigerator, is to encourage some limit to my frequent self-indulgence here. Going out for ice cream may cost more, but because it cuts down on the frequency of my partaking, it helps to make the scale readings at my doctor's appointments a more pleasant experience.

But such a favorable outcome arises out of framing environmental influences in a negative manner. It focuses on what they can help you avoid rather than what your environment might contribute to you in more affirmative ways.

Drawing upon the affirmative dimensions of your settings for reflection requires, first of all, paying a renewed attention to the contemplative spaces you have chosen, whether for a focused deliberation or a leisurely pace of daydreaming. It's only if you look up in the cathedral, appreciate the beauty of a campus, or allow the quiet of a secluded path to infuse your awareness that the affirmative possibilities of your settings emerge.

Paying more perceptive attention to your surroundings may sound simple, but it runs into a well-recognized psychological obstacle. Our attention is overwhelmingly selective. Numerous experiments by psychologists confirm that when participants' attention is directed elsewhere, they miss such obvious occurrences as a person in a gorilla suit or a clown on a unicycle wandering through their vision.

So, developing ways to foster an expansion of your perceptions entails more consciously choosing how you direct your attention. I recall hearing of a monk that when asked what he had done over the years, pointed outside his window and simply said, "I watched that flower grow." While our undertaking here hardly aims for us all to become monks, I will in the upcoming pages ask you to ponder that monk's comment, and to consider what it would mean to your life to improve the richness of your daily perceptions.

Affirmation of Hope

A final quality of any authentic reflection – evident in an open spirit – is that it is implicitly an affirmation of hope. This is because reflection, by its very nature, involves taking another look at things. By virtue of this act of reconsideration, reflection opens up the possibility that any current understanding you hold may not be the last word. Any stepping back to consider your present struggles or dilemmas anew is by itself alive to the potential for positive change.

This is certainly not to say that it is easy. As psychological research shows, belief perseverance is a powerful force in our lives. Getting stuck is an all-too-common experience in everything from our ideas to our jobs to our relationships. Remember my talented friend who, when I asked about leaving a job that frustrated him, replied, "I don't even have the time to think about it."

Getting stuck in this existential way occurs whenever you treat yourself as an object, that is, something predetermined or settled now once and for all. But whatever efforts you may expend in this direction, they never exhaustively work.

This is because we are, by our very nature, not objects but active subjects.

Try a little experiment. Focus your attention on yourself. In your mind's eye, make your perception of yourself fully explicit, rendering as transparent as possible all your features and subtleties. What is missing from this mental picture of yourself? The part of you that *perceives* this picture. Now, focus on the part of yourself doing the perceiving. What occurs? You are able to bring into focus the perceiving part of yourself. But now: What about the part of yourself that perceives this perceiving self? The part of yourself perceiving your perceiving escapes your self-conception. This can go on indefinitely. Your consciousness, by its very nature, is self-transcending.

Our self-transcending nature is the mark of our status as active subjects, our ever-present capacity to see ourselves and our unfolding lives anew. As you shall see as we go on, that means you are never as stuck as it may first seem and that your world is always larger than it initially appears.

***

Looked at in this way, virtue-infused reflection is not an esoteric activity, one requiring technical expertise or open only to a gifted few. It is an everyday practice available to us all and best engaged in on a regular basis.

There is much in our lives that we can't control. We can't control the innate talents we possess, the physical looks we are born with, and many of the circumstances in which we find ourselves.

But we can control the persons we wish to become – and this is where ethics comes in. It is the foundational way we claim our dignity and announce our value.

Every ethical choice we make not only helps to determine who we are to become but, at the same time, transcends ourselves, leaving a mark that remains even after we have moved on. For every such choice we make is an abiding testimony to life's higher possibilities, available to others to reflect upon and extend.

If you're willing to accept an invitation to engage in this distinctive kind of ethical reflection, you can never be sure about the details of where it will lead. In my own experience, there have been my share of detours, wrong turns, and simple pauses in confusion. But while you can't predict with certainty the specifics ahead, you can be sure you'll end up closer to where you need to be.

It's worth the effort. Remember, I intend to argue, an ethical life is an extraordinary life. So, let's begin.

2

Our Relationship with Ourselves

A Holistic Mind

> "The first principle is that you must not fool yourself – and you are the easiest person to fool."
>
> Richard Feynman

Becoming Yourself

It's Complicated

A holistic mind is all about becoming yourself.

In aspiring to a holistic mind, we aim for the virtue that embodies the ethical excellence possible in our relationship with ourselves. At the core of this ethical excellence is the establishment of a self. And being the complicated creatures that Walt Whitman saw us to be, the establishment of self is a complex matter.

Fundamentally, this virtue requires a coherent conception of self – something few of us obtain without effort. For at its best, the coherent self exhibits consistency, constancy, and character. Taken together, these three qualities constitute what we commonly admire as "integrity."

Integrity, for instance, requires consistency. Someone who professes to care deeply about the environment, yet in his daily household routines shirks from efforts to recycle, falls short of the ideal of integrity. Similarly, a boss who one day treats his employees well, but the next day, after getting caught in a traffic jam during his morning commute, arrives moody and is short-tempered with his staff, hardly embodies the constancy we associate with integrity. And since even someone as morally unscrupulous as a common thief can be consistent and constant in his behavior, integrity also requires character, a coherence informed by ethical values.

Seeking your Better Self: Timely Virtues for a Turbulent World, First Edition. Jeffrey Nesteruk.
© 2026 John Wiley & Sons, Inc. All rights reserved, including rights for text and data mining and training of artificial intelligence technologies or similar technologies. Published 2026 by John Wiley & Sons, Inc.

So, the integrity we're after here is more than a splintered, ephemeral identity, shifting from moment to moment. The identity it manifests must be a rooted one, cohering around a set of reflected-upon ethical values, providing evidence of a moral character.

***

Once after I gave a speech, a colleague commented, "It was so you!" Looking back, I'm not sure she meant it as a compliment or as an accusation, but it was clear she thought the speech in some way bore my personal imprint. The self she thought of as "Jeff" was part and parcel of the content and delivery of the speech.

But pinning down the makeup of the "self" she had in mind isn't always a straightforward task.

This is true not only when we consider the other persons we know but also true – perhaps especially true – when we contemplate our own self.

An all-too-common bit of advice in new or stressful situations is simply, "Be yourself." While seemingly straightforward, this advice did little to quell my many wobbly moments as a teenager. Growing up, I was never sure how to square this bit of advice with my experience of my own interior state as complex, conflicted, and often even when I probed, inscrutable. At the time, I identified with a line from one of my favorite Kris Kristofferson songs, the pilgrim as "a walking contradiction, partly true, and partly fiction."

Even as I've gotten older, I'm not sure how much better I've gotten at "being myself."

More than we sometimes wish to admit, we're puzzles that take time, effort, and ingenuity to put together. Such work too is not something once and done, but an ongoing process.

To begin with, it's worth honestly considering how much you are a "walking contradiction." Even a bit of reflection can uncover conflicts among your desires.

First- and Second-order Desires

Consider a distinction that philosophers are fond of – that between first- and second-order desires. Typically, when we consider our desires, we are, if we were to speak more precisely, thinking of our first-order desires. I desire a chocolate ice cream cone. I desire a raise at work. I desire that new car I just saw in the commercial.

But there are also second-order desires. I may want that chocolate ice cream cone, yet at the same time, wish that I didn't as I am trying to cut back on snacks in an effort to lose some weight. If you want something, but wish you didn't, that underlying wish is a second-order desire. Second-order desires are not what you want, but rather what you want to want.

It may sound a bit complicated, but it's really the stuff of everyday life. You may want to curse out that delivery service that screwed up your online order, but wish you were not a person who could so easily lose his patience. You may want to watch that last episode of the Netflix series you been bingeing, but you dearly wish it wasn't so tempting because you have an early meeting tomorrow.

First and foremost, it's because of our differing desires that we have to think about our relationship with ourselves. It's the only way if we hope to put the puzzle together in an abiding and satisfying manner.

Claiming Yourself

From an ethical standpoint, a self is not something pre-given, something you already have, but rather a distinctive kind of personal achievement, one that calls upon your best efforts.

Given what psychologists tell us, you're up against quite a lot.

Mental health counselor and anthropologist Brian J. McVeigh talks about the self as systemized, as serialized, and as dramatized. It's worth taking a closer look at these three ways of thinking about the self, as each in its own way complicates achieving the kind of stable, enduring self that a genuinely ethical life requires.

Systemized Self

At the core of a systemized notion of self is the idea that the self does not have an essential ego, but rather is a dynamic network of internal relationships. Simply put, this is a view of the self in which no one is in charge. As McVeigh explains: It's an illusion that an individual agent "dwelling in our heads, is working the levels. No directing authority is necessary. The individual psyche is a system or collection of subsystems that responds differently depending on social situation ..."

It is easy to be sympathetic with this view because of the way it captures a significant part of our reality. As our internal parts interact, they bring different configurations of the self to the fore. In a talkative group, this may mean you emerge as a listener; in one in which silence reigns, you may take the initiative to start a conversation.

Anyone who's ever been part of a family knows a larger social version of this dynamic. There is the conscientious sibling, the carefree one, the controlling sibling, the accommodating one. The identity of the family emerges from their interaction. You can't understand any of the parts without understanding the whole. A changing or alteration of one part impacts on the entirety of the family. As an individual player in this kind of dynamic, it is challenging to change as the family's expectations have already solidified around the roles each must play.

Serialized Self

In this version of the self, the self does have an autonomous, independent existence, but it is a changing one. There is no constant, underlying core to the self, but rather multiple selves varying with the role or context in which one is engaged. The self relating to one's spouse is different than the self-communicating with one's children. The self at home varies from the self at work. In this regard, some groups frequently report on the need to "code-switch" at work, acting and speaking in a way acceptable to the dominant culture.

Dramatized Self

There is a performance aspect to being a self. While we are all "acting" throughout our day, some roles are more stylized and conscious, freely chosen and presented. I am very much aware of this aspect of myself in the classroom as I attend to how I dress, speak, move, and interact. I must at some level meet students' expectations of a professor, but I also must confound them, offering surprises and thus creating in students' minds an openness to consider anew the possibilities of the classroom.

I remember once listening to a professional actor describe how directors choose an actor for a role with an awareness of the actor's previous roles and the expectations of the actor that have been built up in the public's mind. All will affect the audience's impressions of the actor's current performance.

Students, I'm sure, also imagine all sorts of things, some correct and some not, about me outside of class. Indeed, I probably without realizing it give them all sorts of clues. But in some measure, my success as a teacher depends on these external imaginings reinforcing my self-presentation in the classroom.

Your Ethical Self

Dynamics in Play

Each of these conceptions of the self – systemized self, serialized self, dramatized self – offers insights into the psychological dynamics in play as we go about our day. The systemized self reminds us of the complexity of our internal dynamics. The serialized self prompts reflection about where, and even if, our core self resides. The dramatized self emphasizes the powerful significance of self-presentation in our lives. Shakespeare's not the only one who thought all the world's a stage.

But the formation of an ethical self entails a distinctive challenge. It requires, at a minimum, a stable, enduring self. For without some underlying unity to the self, ethical attribution and judgment lose their everyday significance. If the self is not a persisting entity, any sort of attribution of fault for a past action implicitly absolves the present self that is being subjected to judgment or evaluation. This is because, under a strict notion of the serialized self, agency for the past action resides in a self that no longer exists. The "I" that did it is not the "I" that now stands before you.

Similarly, the systemized view of the self undercuts the individual agency upon which ethics depends. Remember on this view of the self, there is no directing authority. Without an agent in control of conduct freely undertaken, there can be no ethical responsibility, at least as we typically conceive it.

Achieving Your Ethical Self

With this in mind, we can see more clearly the challenge of achieving an ethical self. It is something that calls for the virtue-infused reflection we began to outline and develop in Chapter 1. There we saw how the power of reflection arises from its connection to the four virtues. This deeper, more philosophical reflection can locate your enduring core that persists through the more superficial, serial selves that are part of all our lives. And as we shall see as we go forward, developing your ethical self through this virtue-infused reflection inevitably also includes drawing upon the other three relationships we have beyond ourselves – relationships with others, with things, with that which is greater than ourselves.

For the moment, the dramatized self is key to this ongoing process. For the dramatized self is part of a larger story and this is what enables the self to have a stable, enduring nature. The story you choose to tell about yourself is what gives rise to the coherent self you're aiming for. This narrative integrates the more superficial serial selves so readily seen in your daily routines.

Developing Your Narrative Self

You have to become, as Friedrich Nietzsche put it, a poet of your own life. So, rather than the direction from another – however well intentioned – that you should, "Be yourself," your aspiration for an ethical self needs to come in the form of a kind of self-interrogation, a reflective question in which you ask, "So, what's my story?" Thus, as we go forward, pause regularly, and ask yourself: "What is the story that I wish to tell about myself?" This is the fundamental, underlying task in your undertaking of moral exploration.

As you reflect upon the story you wish to tell about yourself, you're enriching a self that is simply stable and enduring. You are adding to it the two other essential elements for an undertaking aimed at moral exploration and growth. After all, the story you wish to tell is *your* story, so it is *creative*. And because your story will ground and guide your choices, it's a story that is *actionable*, something you can draw upon in your conduct going forward.

As a virtue, the holistic mind aspires to a coherent conception of yourself, a rooted identity, a self-integration establishing your integrity as a person. But this integrity is only the beginning, not the end of your story. In developing your narrative self, you get to choose where that integrity might lead. And that is where everyday virtues, such as a holistic mind, hold their extraordinary promise.

But the self-serving bias to which we are all subject should give you pause here. A healthy dose of humility is in order if ever you see yourself "as better than most" or interpret your world "in self-serving ways."

This is especially true because of the way this exaggerated sense of ourselves extends to our evaluation of our moral character. In one survey, people were asked, "How would you rate your own morals and values on a scale of 1–100 (100 being perfect)?" Half of those responding rated themselves at 90 or above.

Anyone who casually pronounces such a self-rating may want to take another look.

Bringing together the pieces of yourself is, as we noted earlier, first and foremost, about understanding the conflicts among your desires. As we saw with the presence of first- and second-order desires, this relationship has some complexity. And this too will be part of the story you choose to tell about yourself.

The Relationship of Your Desires to Your Own Happiness

Your Pursuit of Happiness

As always, you want to bring your whole self to the endeavor, remembering how a good life – one lived fully – is a life that is both admirable and one you desire. This is certainly part of the self-integration that establishes your integrity as a person.

Thus, in constructing the enduring self that provides a firm basis for your ethical agency, you need to reflect more broadly about the relationship of your desires to your own happiness.

Philosophers have thought a great deal about this subject. Let's consider four different ways to think about your relationship to your desires, allowing at least initially, for the pursuit of happiness to be our guide. Each has a rich philosophic pedigree.

Happiness entails:

1. satisfying your desires
2. having the right desires
3. overcoming your desires
4. but can we ever truly know our desires

Happiness as Satisfying Your Desires

At first blush, getting what you want certainly can seem like the key to happiness. If you're lonely and looking for friends, unexpectedly running into one of them when shopping can be a delight. You might even put the shopping on hold for a bit and grab a cup of coffee together.

It can certainly be a welcome surprise when after a hectic day and arriving home hungry, you discover your roommate already has dinner on the table. When food is something you desire, it tastes extra good. Good meals, whether at a business meeting or on a romantic date, raise everyone's mood.

Whether it's a supportive chat with a friend or indulging in that delicious dessert, getting what you want can contribute to your happiness.

Yet like so many things, the idea that fulfilling your desires is the key to happiness is a bit more complicated than it initially appears. You run into what psychologists call the hedonic treadmill. The basic idea behind the hedonic treadmill is that once you get something, say, a raise at work, it momentarily increases your happiness, but then as you adapt to your enhanced salary, you return to your earlier set level of happiness. You now need yet another higher raise in order to gain a boost in good spirits. It can be a never-ending process, calling to mind a quote attributed to John D. Rockefeller. When posed the question of how much money does it take to make a person happy, he answered, "Just one more dollar."

There is also the problem of diminishing marginal utility, as economists regularly remind us. An extra dollar for a well-to-do adult will not have the same value as for a kid looking longingly at an array of convenience store candy. And even for the most devoted lover of desserts, the tenth cookie will never taste as good as the first.

But there is yet another level of complication.

Happiness as Having the Right Desires

As we saw in our discussion of first- and second-order desires, all desires are not created equal. Indeed, as we recognized, we all have desires that we wish we didn't have. Paradoxically, we have desires that we don't want.

We can be led astray if we simplistically see desires as foundational to who we are. Aristotle famously pointed out how our character is, in an important sense, more fundamental than our desires. This is because a person of good character will desire different things than those of nefarious nature. A bully might desire to humiliate a classmate while a compassionate student might take pleasure in helping another with his math homework.

If some desires are harmful to have – bullies, for instance, seldom find success in any activity requiring trust and voluntary cooperation – then the development of the kind of character that promotes pro-social desires is something worth striving for. Rather than simply aiming to satisfy whatever desires we may have, we need to ask: What are the right desires? In other words, what are the desires that lead to our larger flourishing?

One question that I occasionally pose to my students is: Can a coward be happy? When I do, I receive a mix of responses. Some certainly will say, "Yes." When a coward runs from a difficult situation, he undoubted escapes the immediate stress of dealing with something he would rather avoid. In satisfying this immediate desire, his life may well be more superficially pleasant than the life of one with the fortitude to take on difficult challenges.

Nonetheless, few parents wish to raise their kids to be cowards. Quite the opposite: We hope they develop the character that enables them in challenging circumstances to rise to the occasion.

Happiness Is Overcoming Your Desires
Alternatively, perhaps the path to personal happiness lies in another direction. Not with the ongoing work of developing character and fostering the right desires, but in rooting out desires themselves. Our desires often make us unhappy. In some cases, the unhappiness stems from our desires being frustrated or unfulfilled in some way. Think, for instance, of a romantic rejection or the hoped-for promotion that didn't occur.

In Buddhist thought, there is the concept of detachment or nonattachment, encouraging a freedom from cravings or desires. While in Buddhist thought the idea of detachment or nonattachment has much deeper philosophic roots, most of us recognize in our daily lives the value of stepping back from our desires. We might take a moment when angry before speaking or resist the urge to compulsively check emails when it would interrupt a family outing.

The growing popularity of mindfulness can also foster a reexamination of your desires. There are a variety of techniques associated with mindfulness, from simply finding a quiet place to meditate to a focused set of breathing exercises to body scans attending to your physical sensations. All of these techniques aim to bring you fully into the present moment. In so doing, you gain a renewed awareness of your desires. Such recognition of your desires can itself lessen their power as you discern their shape or locate their source or question their value.

Such awareness can also help you trace the effects of your desires on your thinking, feeling, and action. Tracing these effects illuminates how even the desires you're aware of may affect you in hidden ways. You may think many of your desires, especially the ones you deem inappropriate, remain safely locked away in your private psyche. Yet they often can affect your public actions in ways others recognize, even if you do not. You may, for instance, not be hiding your anger as well as you think.

But Can You Ever Truly Know Your Desires
But such an emphasis on fostering the disposition and skills for deeper reflection risks sidestepping an even more fundamental issue: Can we ever truly know our desires? The weight of psychological research suggests we are notoriously bad at predicting our future affective states. We, for instance, tend to overestimate how happy winning the lottery would make us.

We can see our own inscrutability powerfully reflected in works of literature. One of my all-time favorite short stories is Leo Tolstoy's *The Death of Ivan Ilyich*. It's the story of a lawyer who lived a superficial life of propriety, artifice, and social climbing. It's only when he's suffering from a life-threatening illness that he comes to question his earlier values and ambitions. Only in the moments before his death does he discover what he had actually desired for most of his life.

Having studied and practiced law myself, I suppose I find a special salience for my life in Tolstoy's story. Yet the need to follow social expectations or maintain appearances is part of most of our lives. Amid the swirl of social chatter and popular belief, it's hard to hear your own voice. And, even harder, once hearing it, to act upon it.

Ralph Waldo Emerson once said, "It is easy in the world to live after the world's opinion; it is easy in solitude to live after our own; but the great man is he who in the midst of the crowd keeps with perfect sweetness the independence of solitude."

For those of us without the genius of Emerson, this stance can seem difficult, if not impossible. Yet Tolstoy, while deeply aware of what he was asking, stresses the importance of doing the precarious work of understanding our desires now.

Reflecting Upon Your Desires

Contemplating these various understandings of your desires can be overwhelming. With much to absorb, it can leave you feeling that the theories don't all add up. As with many first steps, you can be left in a bit of a jumble.

At such junctures, I find myself paraphrasing a quote by Ben Zoma: "Who is the wise person? He who can learn from anyone." In engaging in your undertaking of personal reflection, it's best to cast your philosophic net broadly, being open to insights wherever you might potentially find them.

It is also good to remind yourself that as general matter, our lives are always larger than our conceptions of them. If that weren't true, we'd have nothing left to learn. We are all finite, each of us limited in our own particular ways, yet trying to grasp a world of seemingly infinite depth and richness.

Thus, when seeking the insights of the four ways of thinking broadly about your desires, the best approach is not to attempt to arrive at one as the sole repository of wisdom, exclusive of the other three. Each of the four approaches – satisfying your desires, having the right desires, overcoming your desires, and questioning whether you can ever truly know your desires – has something significant and meaningful to say.

Rather, try to approach each theory as providing an important though incomplete account of your desires and their relationship to your happiness. In your process of personal reflection, draw upon each in the ways that individually most resonate with you. When you do so, what do see?

Thus, satisfying some desires are clearly essential to your happiness – certainly, for instance, your desire to breathe, along with such essentials as the desires for food and shelter. But others, say, your desire to get that next promotion at all costs or be accepted at a more prestigious university than your sibling may fall short of being the right desire upon reflection. Some desires too may exhibit compulsive or addictive parts of your personality that you'd be wise to try and overcome. Throughout the process of reflection, a comportment of humility will serve you well. For whether we truly know our desires is an open question.

From Your Desires to Your Thoughts

As an aspiring virtue, a holistic mind expresses the excellence exhibited by the development of a coherent self. Fostering such a coherent self is part and parcel of building the capacity for a deeper, more authentic form of reflection in your life, a virtue-infused reflection. Without personal integrity, attempts at becoming more skilled at reflection will necessarily be halting, tentative, or unstable. A coherence of self is at once a prerequisite and an aspiration of this chapter's virtue. At the start, you have an unreflective, rudimentary identity. Your reflection can then open up a more mature self-conception that bears the considered imprint of where you want to go. You are beginning to tell your story.

As we've seen, developing a more mature self-conception involves grappling with your various desires. As our discussion of first- and second-order desires illustrated, the desiring aspects of ourselves are rarely conflict free. We all may have yearnings, often strong ones, that we wish we didn't have. I sometimes have a wistful reaction when I recall an apocryphal story that Socrates, while surveying all the goods available in a lively marketplace, remarked, "There is so much that I do not want." There are days when, prompted by the temptations of abundant online purchases, that I'm pretty far from living up to that ideal.

Further, expanding your capacity for reflection involves not simply sorting through the conflicts among your desires. It also means developing a broader angle of vision for considering the relationship of your desires to your personal happiness. Does happiness entail satisfying your desires, for example, or having the right desires? The vantage point you adopt will deeply shape your conception of self that emerges.

As adopting such a broader vantage point implies, what is at stake here is not only wrestling with your desires but also grappling with your thoughts. Aspiring to a clarity of thought, you have to think about your thinking. Because this involves negotiating the tricky hazards of motivated reasoning, clarity of thought has a distinctive complexity all its own. As psychological research decisively shows, we all tend to use our thinking to enhance our positive image of ourselves and to confirm what our unreflective selves already believe. But if done in an unreflective manner, the principles we turn to when asked to explain our beliefs may not always line up with the judgments we espouse.

Thus, just as integrity's ideal of self-integration fosters the need to reflect upon the relationship of your desires to your happiness, so this ideal of integrity calls for you to reflect upon the relationship of your principles to your judgements. As always, we are trying to put the pieces of ourselves together.

The Relationship of Your Principles to Your Judgements

Reflective Equilibrium

Philosopher John Rawls coined the term "reflective equilibrium." This concept has been developed and critiqued in many ways, but here we will focus on its core idea. Reflective equilibrium is state of mind at which your principles match your judgments and your judgments match your principles. We make judgments all the time. If we're pressed on why we judged an action or situation the way we did, our response can take the form of a principle. Thus, if a driver speeds by you when you are out taking a morning walk, you might express annoyance, calling that driver "unsafe." (I've been known to use less refined language). If asked to justify your claim that the driver rushing by was "unsafe," you might say drivers that fail to follow the posted speed limits are unsafe. In doing so, you would be stating a principle: "Safe drivers always obey the speed limit." As the driver that irked you during your morning walk was exceeding the speed limit, your principle is the rationale for your judgement that the driver was unsafe.

But suppose there was more to the driver's situation than you were originally aware. Suppose, for example, you later learned that the driver had just heard from his elderly mother who lives alone, that she had fallen and urgently needed his help. You might also recall that while breaking the speed limit, the driver was careful to give you a wide berth and obeyed the stop sign in front of him. You might well then revise your initial judgment and now consider him a safe driver. But if you were challenged by someone citing the principle you earlier drew upon as a rationale for your original judgment, you would have to modify your original safe driver principle, perhaps saying, "Safe drivers generally obey the speed limit, except in emergencies."

This sort of back-and-forth between principles and judgments is the process of achieving reflective equilibrium. Making the practice of reflective equilibrium a regular part of your ongoing process of reflection can be a powerful way of clarifying your beliefs and judgments. In doing so, you help to forge an integration of your thinking that is a mark of integrity.

Contradiction as the Stimulus for Personal Growth

Early on in my career as a professor, I learned the productive role that encountering a contradiction can play. So much of my scholarly writing in ethics has its origins in some felt tension or friction that I first had to struggle to articulate more fully and then had to resolve or accommodate in some way. It's when something didn't add up that I had to think things through more deeply and comprehensively.

This was true not only in my own scholarly writing but also in the classroom dynamics with my students. Only when students run into some contradiction in the way they are seeing things does a need to reconsider their thinking arise. Such a contradiction is a check on the unreflective nature of motivational reasoning that strives only to confirm prior beliefs. That's when real education can begin.

I also learned that it was remarkably easy to bring to students' awareness some contradiction in their thinking as we explored the controversies of the day. This was not because of any extraordinary skill I had as a teacher. It's because all of us, in ways we can be reluctant to admit, are bundles of contradictions. When I consider further Walt Whitman's statement of "I contain multitudes," I see how it may reveal more than the poetic richness to our lives. It also attests to the struggles life's choices present to us.

Some Exercises

Let's try some exercises aiming for reflective equilibrium. As we engage in reflection more deeply, our goal is for our principles to match our judgments and for our judgments to match our principles. In the process, both principles and judgments are subject to revision. We may adjust our principles to our judgments and adjust our judgments to our principles. If done well, this process of reflection can foster clarity of thought and the development of a more coherent self. In each case, we begin with a principle.

Tell the Truth

Truth-telling is a principle most of us would endorse at least initially. It's something we try to teach our children, something we aspire to in a courtroom setting, and something we criticize in politicians whenever they fall short.

But the prescription to tell the truth is also a principle we regularly violate in small and even large ways. For example, as our parents did with us, my wife and I initially taught our daughter to believe in Santa Claus. (There was also Elf on the Shelf but that's another story. I still recall the tipsy stools as we struggled to find new and creative spots to place the Elf around our house).

In our judgment it was acceptable, even laudatory, for us to tell our daughter Santa exists, even though this violates the principle of truth-telling as Santa Claus does not (I hope this isn't a spoiler for anyone) actually exist. So, seeking reflective equilibrium, we'd have to revise our principle. We might say: Tell the truth, except to children. As there is much in life that kids aren't ready to absorb, this might make sense in a number of circumstances.

My father even employed a more sophisticated approach as we grew older and challenged him on Santa Claus' existence. He still held to the principle of truth-telling, but explained he never violated that principle in making Santa's existence a delightful part of our childhood. For, as he put it, Santa does exist, not as a bearded man in a red suit, but as a spirit, one of love and generosity that marks the holiday season. He thus kept the principle, but argued for a revised judgment regarding his sharing with his kids the story of Santa Claus.

Most of us, however, also fall short of truth telling in our interaction with adults, even if only when attempting to be polite. I'm not the only one, I'm sure, who has complimented a party host on the meal the host served even if it was not especially to my liking. So, the principle of telling the truth, except to children would have to be revised by including lying to adults at least on some occasions.

But such relatively minor falsehoods accompany much more serious yet potentially justifiable deceptions. You wouldn't, for instance, reveal the location of an abused spouse to that spouse's abuser, readily instead choosing to lie. Or, to cite an example many individuals would see as a grayer area: Would you tell someone who answered your ad for the used car you were selling that they were "getting a great deal" if you knew a neighbor one street over was selling the same car for less?

Of course, you could justify withholding the location of an abused spouse by a more general revision of the truth-telling principle: Tell the truth unless it would cause significant harm. But how would such a principle apply to the claim that your used car buyer was "getting a great deal"? Was paying a bit more for a car he wanted a "significant harm"? How, by the way, would you define "harm"? Would it matter that balancing that harm was the benefit your daughter might receive because the sale of your used car would enable you to better manage her college tuition bill due this month?

Over time, through the practice of reflective equilibrium, you can develop a habit that will serve you well. Especially with difficult individuals or in contentious situations, knowing where you stand and being able to articulate why in a principled way can be a game-changer.

Keep Your Promises and Treat Everyone Equally

The same sort of back-and-forth between principle and judgment can occur with other generally accepted injunctions such as keep your promises or treat everyone equally. The more you practice it, the more it clarifies your thinking.

In a personal context, should you keep your promise of fidelity to a spouse who has been unfaithful to you? In a commercial environment, are you obligated to meet your promised delivery dates to your customer if your supplier failed to honor his? How would you alter the promise-keeping principle to maintain consistency with your judgments here?

Many years ago, before I became a parent, students used to tell me they knew I didn't have any children, even though I had never discussed this with them. When I asked why, they said, "We know because whenever you tell us to do something, you always give a reason." At the time, I didn't see that as much of a special virtue.

Now, having become a parent and having shared the challenges (along with the joys) of parenthood, I understand what gave rise to my students' insightful perception. Who among parents dealing with young children hasn't, when challenged at a frustrating moment, said impatiently, "Because I said so!"

For older parents, the issue of inheritances often looms large. As a lawyer, I've frequently encountered parents expressing the belief of treating all their children equally. But what if some are well-off and others are not? What if one child has a particular disability or health concern? What if through the luck of the draw, one had a bad marriage or through no fault of his own lost his job in an unexpected downsizing? How to make these judgments in a principled way? Adhering to the ideal of reflective equilibrium can help to illuminate the way.

Personalizing Reflective Equilibrium

Now that I've shared a bit more of my story, including my failure to consistently live up to my principled aspirations as a young father, I'd like you to give it a try. Spoiler alert: My daughter, now a mature young woman, turned out wonderful! If you're an older parent, I hope your kids did too. If you have younger kids, hang in there.

Take some time and bring to mind your own most wobbly moments – occasions in which your certainty about the right course of action faltered, times when you simply weren't sure what to do. Even more broadly, you might consider a transitional stage in your life when you confronted the question, "And now what?" and in your struggles, you drew a blank.

It could be on the personal front: Is there a friend who let you down? A sibling whose partner treats you poorly? An Instagram post that embarrasses you? A neighbor whose politics you find repugnant? Someone you have to ask for forgiveness? Someone whose favor you failed to return?

It could be in the professional realm: Do you deserve to love your job? What to do about that annoying coworker? When is the right time to retire? Should I take the risk of starting a new business venture?

It could be in your public role: Should you run for the school board? Challenge your tax assessment? Volunteer at that women's shelter? Vote differently? Change your mind about a popular political candidate? Talk more with people who disagree with you?

In whatever wobbly moments you chose to examine, how were you able to resolve them in a principled way? What principles did you turn to? Did they match your judgments? Do you follow such principles throughout your life?

The key to developing the skill of reflective equilibrium is, like so many things, practice. Then practice. Then more practice. The more I do it, the more I recognize its value, having discovered unexpected insights along the way.

***

You've now been introduced to the task of establishing yourself. Who you are is never something simply given, nor even definitively settled. You are always a work in progress with choices to make.

As I stressed in introducing a virtue-infused form of reflection, we are leaving Facebook's old harried dictum behind. As we proceed, you should indulge yourself in lingering over any insights you find particularly intriguing along the way. See them as signals for the work you might wish to do. This deeper, more philosophical form of reflection involves an ongoing commitment to an always unperfected practice. It's a step-by-step endeavor that can at times be uncomfortable but is always infused with new possibilities. Marked by an essential openness, virtue-infused reflection is inherently a hopeful enterprise.

Topical Reflections

We now turn from a broad overview of the challenges and opportunities in our relationship with ourselves to take a more granular perspective. The examples are mine, but in the questions that follow each topical reflection, you have the opportunity to make them your own.

Remember *Seeking Your Better Self* is a book about how to engage in ethical reflection. First broadly: What are your moral values? What is most important to you? How would you define a good life? And then: How to bring these values into your daily choices, encounters, and relationships. That's what the topical reflections now aim to do.

***

In the essay on "Joy" below, consider the difference it might make to our anxious student if she was aware of the difference between first- and second-order desires as she struggles with happiness and success. If you had the chance, what would you tell her about the value of having the right desires?

Joy

A student once told me, "I don't need to be happy – just successful."

At the time, I let it pass – students, after all, regularly say surprising things. Indeed, I like this quality in their conversations. Their talk is unpredictable in a way that's entirely appropriate to the persons-in-process they are.

But this assertion – "I don't need to be happy – just successful" – has an unsettling quality to it once you let it seep in and begin to think about it. It's disconcerting because the student dismisses happiness and does so in such a perfunctory way. It's as if she's saying, "Let's get on to the important stuff."

And the important stuff – professional success – produces an odd juxtaposition. She needn't be happy – "just successful." She places one in opposition to the other.

She's not alone in her feeling. At a workshop for college professors, I listened to a drama professor describe an acting class in which he asked students to write about times in their lives when they had experienced strong emotions, such as anger or jealousy. The emotion they found hardest to convey? Joy.

The words of students often reveal something deeper and broader. They are sensitive barometers of unrecognized trends. Today's expressions of tomorrow's practices. Their words can thus be the visible signs of the less visible struggles encountered by us all.

I have a memory from my own undergraduate years – the headline of my campus newspaper reading, "Why Aren't We Happy?" As the headline suggests, we fell far short of leading joyful lives. Yet at least in my memory, happiness was then still on the agenda. What underlies the tendency of many of us, like my success-seeking student, to give up genuinely trying?

I've often failed to enjoy Sunday because of my schedule on Monday. At bottom, it was simply anticipatory anxiety over the work of the week ahead – fear of arrangements falling through or unexpected complications or my failure to measure up to some challenge in some way. Usually, when Monday came, I did quite well. Much of what I worried about never happened.

Yet each unrealized fear had an effect. It became a silent partner in my success. Linked to my accomplishment and hardened into a habit, it exacted its costs behind the scenes.

Joy has its own moral underpinning. There's a completeness to joy that does not allow us to exclude our sense of the person we should be. Pleasure is certainly possible in less-than-honorable actions. But the experience of joy requires more: it is pleasure taken in worthy things.

The trick behind joy is to desire the desirable – genuinely wanting what is genuinely good. This way the satisfaction of one part of yourself needn't mean the dissatisfaction of another.

For my success-stressed student, such a pleasure is impossible. The choice she makes – not needing to be happy, just successful – creates a division in herself that dissolves the self-integration joy requires. She divorces her pleasure from the achievement she regards as worthy, severing her immediate desires and her higher aspirations.

Of course, creating the integration joy requires is no small task. Indeed, it is a large endeavor, even over a lifetime. Choices must develop into habits that evolve into character.

This means work – work we can't delegate to subordinates or ask of friends. And such work takes time – time we can't compress even with the instant couplings of the Internet.

But the essential first step is trying to live a less fearful life – one that avoids collapsing life's possibilities before exploring them. It entails welcoming uncertainty. It means being comfortably incomplete.

My success-starved student is *un*comfortably incomplete; anxious over what she is not. She has too many silent partners. Never given voice but always present, each fear is having its effect, costing more than it produces.

I wish I could tell her how much I enjoy my Sundays now.

Personal Reflection Prompts

1. Is there a tension in your own life between "success" and "happiness"? When I see my students, such an opposition seems at once odd and unsettling, yet all-too-common. What do you think is going on here? If pressed, how do you suspect the student would define "success"? Define "happiness"?
2. Is joy no longer on the agenda for yourself"? Your friends? Your colleagues? If so, why? If not, what's your secret?
3. As the essay reveals, I've struggled with "anticipatory anxiety." I still at times find it hard to feel that I will be successful in an endeavor without ample amounts of prior worry. Is this something you share? I had a friend in graduate

school that before she would go on any big trip, she would "pre-worry," meticulously anticipating anything possible that could go wrong. Then, if it did, she was able to calmly handle it. Is this a good way to live? For those of us who struggle with anticipatory anxiety, should we try on occasion to simply jump into a new experience, without exposing it to enervating prior analysis? Would doing so help us learn to trust our ability to handle the unexpected? Is this something you'd be willing to try?
4. The essay suggests a necessary underpinning for joy is "to desire the desirable – genuinely wanting what is genuinely good." There is an echo here of this chapter's discussion of Aristotle and the connection between happiness and having the right desires. Similarly, in the book's introduction, we took note of the possibility of "worthy desires," wanting to act in a way that is praiseworthy. Why is this often so hard?
5. The essay also suggests that prior work is needed to experience joy and that such effort "takes time." Do you agree that the ability to lead a joyful life requires a significant measure of internal work and personal growth? Even if true, does this miss the spontaneous moments of joy? Are you, as C.S. Lewis proclaimed, ever "surprised by joy"? What did you learn from such an experience?
6. If you are fortunate enough to experience joy in your life, how do you share that experience with others? Is there a secret sauce to joy that you can communicate to others? Or is it something that everyone must learn on their own? Must you be careful about expressing your joy to others? Would it make them feel better or worse?

***

This next essay brings into sharp relief the internal turmoil we often feel, especially if we are compulsive problem-solvers. If we aspire to develop a coherent concept of self, what steps does a compulsive problem-solver need to take? If this involves a lifelong commitment, how can you comfortably engage in an always unperfected practice?

Stress

Some days, my life feels like a jigsaw puzzle that someone just dropped on the floor. All the pieces are scattered and I no longer see how they fit together.

Not that this keeps me from trying. I'm a compulsive puzzle-solver. Always trying to get everything done, always trying to keep everyone happy. For someone like me, the lack of a desired fit is the quintessence of stress.

This has meant that stress has been a regular companion of mine over the years. Even when I'm relaxing, it lurks in the background. For life has a dynamism that never lets us solve its most basic challenges once and for all. It has a way of knocking the puzzles we thought we had finished to the floor, scattering their pieces.

Lately, I've been asking myself: Why do I have this need to have everything in my life perfectly in place? This need only seems to highlight pieces I wish were there but can't lay my hands on.

So much of the stress in my life arises from my desire for certainty. The fear I've always had that what I don't know *can* hurt me. Rationally, I know this fear is unfounded. The unknowns in my future needn't be horrible; they can be wonderful. After all, some of the unknowns in my past have ended up being delightful surprises.

At bottom, I'm discovering something is wrong with my underlying picture of life as a puzzle to be put together. This picture misses all the mysteries in life to which we ultimately surrender. It blocks the wisdom that can be found in life's ill-fitting moments.

The thing to remember is that jigsaw puzzles are at their best *before* they're put together. They're at their best, that is, when they're still puzzles. In their unfinished form, they have the ability to engage and inspire us, to keep us open and inquiring. The heightened awareness we have when we're doing a puzzle begins to dissipate once we're done.

The key to managing stress is to recognize this feature in life's larger puzzles. In a fundamental way, the lack of fit in our lives fits us. It is not something we should try to escape. Through it, our deeper philosophic character emerges, allowing us to experience life's puzzles as puzzling, helping us toward the virtue of knowing when we do not know.

Approaching our lives in this radical way involves trade-offs, to be sure. It means accepting more uncertainty, getting comfortable with less control. But in so many ways, this is giving up things we never genuinely had. In a delightful manner, it's getting something for nothing.

Thus, the jigsaw puzzle that's been knocked to the floor is more than the loss it initially seems to be. Admittedly, the mastery of a moment ago is no longer readily on display. But the puzzle can now demonstrate its own distinctive excellence. It offers us the chance to encounter anew something not yet put together, to come to know once again that we have more to learn.

And in its distinctive excellence, the puzzle offers us the possibility of a different kind of mastery: not of it, but of ourselves.

Personal Reflection Prompts

1. Does your life ever feel like "a jigsaw puzzle that someone just dropped on the floor"? In this chapter focused on our relationship with ourselves, we brought to the fore the tensions within ourselves, tensions flowing from the

complexities of our own desires and compounded by the contradictions in our own thinking. It's easy to see how Walt Whitman's celebration of "containing multitudes" can some days feel like more of a curse than a blessing.
2. What is your first reaction when something doesn't go the way you expected? Is it frustration? Fear? Then, what is your second reaction? Do you ever feel intrigued or curious? Do you ever find satisfaction in solving an unexpected problem?
3. Are you a "compulsive problem solver," trying to "keep everyone happy"? A friend of mine is the person everyone in his family turns to when a difficult situation or occurrence arises and requires resolution. As he readily admits, he finds great satisfaction in the role. But others might feel unfairly burdened or taken advantage of. Are you the person others turn to when a problem arises? Is it a role you've chosen or has it been thrust upon you? Doesn't the nature of the problem matter? Good listeners aren't necessarily good mechanics. Someone who loves cooking may not relish having to look after your children in a pinch.
4. Do you tend to experience what is uncertain or unknown as threatening or harmful? Why do you feel that way? Has it served you well? Conversely, did you ever have an unknown in your life turn out to be "wonderful"? One of my favorite poets, Rita Mae Brown, has a line about possibilities, using the metaphor of a door. "The door itself makes no promises," she writes, "It is only a door." The future intrinsically has that quality – it doesn't guarantee what follows will be good or bad, but only that something will follow. It is worth reflecting on why you view the future in whatever way you do.
5. Is there a "virtue" in "knowing when we do not know"? Socrates certainly thought so, but such a view seems out of sync with our hyperconnected world with so much information readily available with the keystroke of a computer. We will consider this further in the chapter on our relationship with that which is greater than ourselves, exploring the virtue of an open spirit.
6. This essay also points to the mastery that is at the core of this chapter's virtue of a holistic mind, the mastery of ourselves. This "different kind of mastery" is receiving a diminishing focus in our colleges as students understandably wish to develop the "job ready" skills that lead to steady jobs and secure careers. Such skills range from marketing to engineering to welding to counseling. But with a diminishing focus on self-mastery, will they be able to use those skills well?

***

As we have described it, a virtue-infused form of reflection focuses not simply on what you do, but more fundamentally, on who you are. That is why it necessarily draws upon your ethical core, tapping virtues such as a holistic mind. The following essay asks whether boredom has a positive role to play in fostering this deeper, more authentic form of reflection.

Boredom

I've been thinking a lot lately about how much we spend on fun. I've watched TVs get bigger, vacations more exotic, hobbies more consuming. We no longer expect our free time to be free.

With so much invested, there's a loss of leisure in our search for amusement. When we pay more, we expect more. We get serious about our fun.

With this ever-expanding search for entertainment, I worry we've forgotten something simple but true: There's a virtue to boredom.

Contrary to popular expectations, boredom is not always something we should avoid. It is rather something for which we should cultivate a healthy tolerance. A measure of comfort with boredom is a habit worth developing because we need to be able to pause in our lives if we are to experience them fully.

Were we to slow down, we would discover this: We are today overstimulated and therefore underappreciative. We miss out on life's more subtle pleasures.

Now, I'm not saying we should give up all our toys. I enjoy Netflix too much to let it go completely. My thought is a much more modest one. I think we should strive for an adult version of the "quiet time" we try to teach to kids. Adults too need a time in their day when their only amusement is their own imagination.

It is difficult to see a positive side to boredom, particularly for high-achievers. This is because high-achievers tend to recognize only the most debased form of boredom. In this vulgar form, boredom arises from a defect in character, such as laziness or disengagement. In our get-ahead world, it is not the mark of someone destined for success.

I remember a high school friend who exemplified this form of boredom. He had the most peculiar effect on me. I could be enjoying my day, eagerly engaged in whatever I was doing, yet when he'd stopped by, I'd begin to lose interest in my endeavor. Whatever I was doing was never enough for him, and his dissatisfaction was contagious. Inevitably, my interaction with him interfered with the pleasure I took in my own activity.

If all we see is this common conception of boredom, its virtue is invisible. My high school friend's boredom was rooted in an adolescent dissatisfaction with himself. It was one that continually led him to look outward rather than inward. It required a lifestyle built on distractions. He asked from other persons what he could never give himself. Even though understandable in adolescence, this is hardly a model to which we should aspire as adults.

But as adults, there is a richer possibility before us. This richer possibility is a boredom we can choose to allow into our lives once we've grown comfortable with ourselves. Comfortable enough to abstain from our amusements. Comfortable enough to take an undistracted look inward.

Indeed, I've found the more comfortable I am with boredom, the more interesting I become. When I distance myself from my high-tech distractions, I discover the deeper parts of myself only stillness can bring to fruition. The strength underlying my moments of weakness. The joy that survives my disappointments. The hope that always wants to try again.

The virtue of boredom is the way it challenges you to this deeper understanding of yourself. For with all the pleasure our amusements bring, they can also reduce us to our most superficial selves. They can pretty-up our vices, adorn our fears, render our insecurities almost invisible. They can keep us from the more authentic persons we are capable of becoming.

This steady stream of high-priced amusements in our lives has an obvious financial cost. ATVs, wine cellars, and Jacuzzis rarely come cheap. But the deeper, personal cost of these amusements may be harder to discern. They can turn our adulthood into a distorted adolescence. If we let too many of them into our lives, we risk becoming older versions of my high school friend, always looking outward rather than inward and finding that whatever we are doing, it is never enough.

Personal Reflection Prompts

1. This chapter's discussion of the "hedonic treadmill" might engender a bit of reflection on "how much we spend on fun." For as "TVs get bigger, vacations more exotic, hobbies more consuming," we see our desires fully on display. Yet the hedonic treadmill phenomenon should give us pause in too blithely adopting a conception of happiness as entailing the satisfaction of our desires. Have you ever experienced buyer remorse where a desired purchase failed to bring the lasting pleasure you expected?
2. What do you see as "life's more subtle pleasures"? What pleasures for you involve little or no financial cost? Can different kinds of pleasure interfere with each other? Does the large TV come with a loss of family conversation?
3. Are there different kinds of boredom? Can you be bored in different ways? Should at least some types of boredom be criticized or discouraged?
4. Is there, as the essay suggests, a virtue to boredom? Would you advocate an adult "quiet time"? What would that look like in your own life? Given your responsibilities, is such a quiet time even possible in your life? And if not, what should you do about that?
5. Achieving a holistic mind does need the concentration of an inward turn. But how do you develop the distinctive comfortableness that inward turn

requires? How does one become, as the essay puts it, "[c]omfortable enough to abstain from our amusements"?
6. One of my scientist friends says, "Boredom is a choice." As this essay details, all sorts of choices are available to us in this regard. What choices are you making?

***

Virtue-infused reflection certainly does require, as the essay below puts it, living your life "inside out." But living life in an "inside out" manner depends upon establishing a self that exhibits, as this chapter notes, consistency, constancy, and character. How might the exercise of reflective equilibrium help you develop this type of "integrity"?

Work

I've had an unbalanced work life. I've asked too much of my work and too little of it.

I've asked too much the times I've confused my identity with my job. Early in my career, I could have been one of those high-level executives who after having lost his job, still put on his business suit each morning and left his home in a car he could no longer afford. Keeping his dignity through keeping up appearances.

I could have been one of those fellows because I approached my life in a similar way. Like the executives, I was living life from the outside in rather than from the inside out.

But this is a dangerous strategy. It exposes you to the risk of being nothing more than your external circumstances. And such circumstances change. Just ask the executives.

Despite the danger, many of us approach life this way. This is evident even in our most casual conversations. Upon meeting someone for the first time, we often ask of him what he does, thinking we're discovering who he is. But we have things backward here. Our careers should grow out of our identities, not the other way around.

The skill we need more of is learning how to live life from the inside out. This is a difficult skill, to be sure. But it gets easier the more you practice it.

A great place to begin is by bringing yourself to work.

I've asked too little of my job whenever I've failed to bring myself to work. Not that I was physically absent, but I've left behind my fundamental character. Our basic values slip easily away from us at work. On the job, we take actions we've taught our children not to do, rationalizing our conduct as "just business." We play the kind of politics that's made us cynical about our professional politicians. More than we would wish, we smile at people we don't like, say things we don't believe. Thus, while we may make it to the top, the person who arrives there is fundamentally different from ourselves.

Success at work depends fundamentally on your ability to bring your genuine self to work. You need to find something you see as having intrinsic value in what you do. Something you'd do even if you were paid not to do it. If all of your job has only an instrumental value, you will never bring your talents fully to it. Your passion for it will be lacking. You will do only what is necessary to get things done, which is rarely enough to do things well.

Even when you succeed, the rewards will all be external. And when the rewards are only external, they're never enough. Just ask those laid-off executives.

My out-of-balance work life was rooted in fear. Fear of accepting the challenge of living from the inside out. Living from the inside out requires a starting place, a core at the center of yourself that you unconditionally trust. I asked too much of work when I was afraid to find that core. I've asked too little of work when I lacked the courage to let it out.

Our Silicon Valley culture breeds many fears. Fear of not working hard enough. Fear of missing out. Fear of selling out. Fear of being the person who's only worth 10 million while his peers are worth twenty.

But the most dangerous fear the culture breeds is the fear of a serenity within ourselves, of a core we can always trust.

We often complain superficially about our jobs but rarely think deeply about them. We're engrossed in them without being soulfully involved.

When we'd rather work than reflect, we forget that reflection is necessary to do our work well. This is not an ivory tower ideal. It is the most practical of necessities. Corporations regularly pay consultants good money to do the thinking they don't have time to do.

We resist thinking deeply about work because it is so difficult. Indeed, the changes in the workplace we otherwise value make it harder still. For these changes reduce our time and space for reflection by spilling our workday over into the rest of our lives. Casual dress and telecommuting break down the barriers between work and home. With cell phones, you are never away from your desk. Work for a virtual organization and you are virtually always there.

Plus, if you want to think deeply about work, you need to think about more than work. For the significance of what you do lies in the broader life you lead. Connections between your work and your better self come to fruition only if work is properly situated.

The first step of reflection is finding a home for your work within your higher ideals and deeper relationships. Work is at its best when it's part of the better part of you.

The more you bring out the core of yourself that you trust unconditionally, the more possibilities of connection you will discover. Living life from the inside out, you can find a new dignity in your endeavors.

Personal Reflection Prompts

1. Do you live life from the inside out or from the outside in? However you approach this dichotomy, is your approach something you consciously chose? What examples from your own life might you use to illustrate how you see yourself in this regard? Is it possible to live life totally from the inside out? Would such a life be desirable?
2. Do you have a core within yourself that you can always trust? How would you describe that core? What enables you to trust it?
3. Do you have an unbalanced work life? If so, how did that come about? Is this something you'd like to change? Do you view it as possible to change?
4. In what ways in your life is it important to you to keep up "appearances"? Can you give some examples? What would be the consequences if you failed to keep up one or more of these appearances? Would it matter if your children learned the reality behind these appearances? If your spouse? If your friends? If your work colleagues? If your parents?
5. Have you ever engaged in something ethically questionable at work? In the way you treated colleagues? In the way you handled finances? In the secrets that you kept? In the way you met targeted goals? Conversely, have you ever been treated unethically by others? Why did you let that occur?
6. Do you believe success at work entails bringing your "genuine self" to work? Is it important to find "intrinsic value" in what you do? What in your work are you passionate about? Are there dangers in asking too much from your work?

***

This essay raises the issue of whether achieving a coherent sense of self allows for the acceptance of aspects of yourself that you wish were otherwise. Put even more pointedly, can forgiveness be an integral feature of the consistency you aim for?

Mistakes

You can spend a lifetime learning how to make mistakes.

When I was younger, I was less aware of my failings. Now easing into middle age, I'm more aware of my failings, but also paradoxically, more accepting of them. I've learned that self-acceptance can occur far short of perfection.

When you're young, you can't really make mistakes. So few of the choices you make are actually irreversible. This is part of the reason we so readily forgive mistakes made earlier in life. We call them "youthful indiscretions."

But as I get older, I see my mistakes differently. I have less time to make things right.

It's not that I'm yet old enough to have regrets of the most serious kind – those that can no longer be rectified or compensated for in some way. For in my middle years, there are few choices that have been ruled out completely. I can still go back to college, learn to skydive, start a new business, have a son. But I can now see for the first time in my life a point where such things will no longer be possibilities. I can envision my experience contracting rather than expanding. I can imagine getting old.

My middle-age mistakes do frustrate me more than my youthful indiscretions in one way: I now see how there are particular kinds of mistakes I do over and over again. I shouldn't pick up the phone at dinner time, but I still do. Never learning any better.

But even here, I am helped by the people who accept me as I am. My wife, Hedi, forgives my repetitive failings, and I try to respond in kind. We like to say "Between the two of us, there's always one fully functioning adult in the household." And that's enough.

I suppose you could say the missteps of my more mature self should bother me more. After all, the mistakes I make now have broader consequences. When I was younger and single, my mistakes were mostly self-inflicted wounds. Now, as a married man with a daughter, I have more people depending on me. I can do more harm.

I also have more people looking up to me, and thus can more be the source of disappointments. With my students, I've become a role model. Even after many years of teaching, this still surprises me. I can't yet see myself through their eyes.

So, the gaps in my middle-age life have a salience they did not years before. I can't avoid the daily distance between my ideals and my actions.

But the salience of these gaps has become encased in a larger significance. These gaps are no longer strangers. They have acquired an intimacy over time.

I remember my mother saying, "You can't choose your family." My faults are like that. There are parts of myself I wouldn't have chosen.

But I've learned to forgive them in the way I do my family members. You need to forgive whatever is part of yourself.

Even when it takes a lifetime.

Personal Reflection Prompts

1. This essay suggests we look differently at mistakes depending on when they occur in a lifetime. We are, for example, more likely to regard mistakes occurring earlier in life as "youthful indiscretions." This view has a particular salience for me as I wrote this essay a while back and, reading it now, I see subtle shifts in my thinking. In the course of your life, have you changed the

way you regard your mistakes? How so? Are you more accepting of them or less? Do you expect the way you currently see your mistakes to change in the future?
2. Did you ever commit what you first regarded as a mistake and later came to view it as the right decision or action? That is to say, have you ever been mistaken about a mistake? Consider this in relation to this chapter's virtue of a holistic mind. Should a holistic mind be an unchanging mind?
3. Is it ever important to let others make their own mistakes? Are there things individuals can only learn well through making mistakes? More broadly, do you see benefits in making mistakes? What are they? If you've ever been in a position of authority – say as a parent or manager or student leader – do you ever let those under your supervision make mistakes?
4. I know an attorney who if he sees another attorney making a mistake, he will point the mistake out to the other attorney, rather than take advantage of it. He says, "It's only professional." Is this what it means to be a member of a profession?
5. How do you deal with the parts of yourself that you "wouldn't have chosen"?
6. As my wife and I do, do you rely on others to compensate for your less-than-ideal moods or moments? Do you reciprocate in return? Does this help to foster intimacy? Does it ever cause resentment?

***

In its own way, this essay reasks a question we posed earlier in this chapter: Can we ever truly know our desires? If our weariness stems from our desire to meet on our own all the demands and expectations we encounter, we may miss our need for rest and, even more fundamentally, our desire for others who will care for us, even when we can't reciprocate.

Weariness

I had my tires checked the other day and the proprietor told me they were good for a few more months. I thought to myself: My tires are doing better than I am. Their treads have a ways to go. I'm feeling worn out.

I'm tired – in an uncomfortable way. It's a restless weariness. It's a tiredness coupled with the feeling that I should be doing more.

I know why. I've been missing my mark a lot lately. Not doing things as well as I had hoped for or intended. I have a student who wants a better class. A colleague who wants shorter meetings. A friend who expects me to call more often. And, at some level, they're all right.

But it's a right that doesn't fit together. A right that at a deeper level is wrong.

Over the years, I've learned that weariness has within itself its own roots of rejuvenation. But you have to dig for them. Often, they're not exposed until your tiredness has left you nowhere else to go. Until you're so tired you don't have the energy to go anywhere else. And then, finally, you're in the place that you should be.

But most of us fight getting there – fight it sometimes with a passionate intensity. We want to believe we can solve problems by doing more – more for our families, more for our work, more for the wider world around us.

It's at this point that our weariness becomes most worrisome. There's a destructive dynamic at work here. One that's taking us away from where we need to be.

What we need – is rest. That's the beginning of rejuvenation. But feeling we should be doing more can only leave us restless.

The kind of rest we need depends on the kind of tired we are.

The easiest kind of tiredness to deal with is a physical weariness. Just sleep late. Take a nap. Put your feet up.

There is also a tiredness of the intellect. It's when you don't want to take in another problem, consider another perspective, listen to something you haven't heard before. Here you need to turn your personal information switch to "Off." Stop trying to take things in. Take a walk. Stare off into space. Even watching a bad sitcom can be a relief. Nothing to feel guilty about here. Remember the "Off" switch is also the "On" switch. You can't have one without the other.

Harder to deal with is an emotional tiredness – where you feel you don't want to feel, at least for a while. It's when you need to be unconnected if you're ever going to be connected again. It could be with a particular person. It could be with everyone. But it can't be ignored. The thing to remember here is that it won't always be this way – and believe it.

The trick is to do more of less. Doing more of less is hard because most of us have a hard time being easy on ourselves.

I may have trouble finding time to get new tires over the next few months, but I'm not worried because my wife has said she'd do it. Earlier in my life, I wouldn't have been comfortable with that. But in the last few years of marriage, I've learned how to rely on someone else.

Relying on someone else is also the key when you're dealing with more than buying new tires – when you're dealing with the deeper kinds of weariness I've mentioned.

It's the key because relying on someone else is the way to do more of less.

I've discovered there are people in my life who will call me back even if I forget to return their calls. They're special people. Because of them I know that even when I stop, they'll take care of things. I can let go without fear of getting lost.

We are never perfect alone. Solitary imperfection is built into our nature. You can begin to do more of less when you learn that such imperfection is not your lack but your luster. It's your luster because it's what connects you to others.

And what connects others to you. I think I might surprise my wife by getting some new tires put on *her* car. I've noticed hers are beginning to show their wear. In strange and wonderful ways, new tires can add to more than the life of your vehicle.

Personal Reflection Prompts

1. Have you felt tired lately? What kind of tired? Physical? Intellectual? Emotional? Maybe all three? Together or separately, they all give rise to tensions within ourselves that are hard to overcome.
2. Are there other kinds of weariness in your life? You could be tired of an argument that goes on and on without any satisfying resolution or even progress. You could be tired of a criticism you continually hear. Especially one that's unfair. You could be tired of a person or a place or a habit you can't seem to shake. Even quite minor things, if they persist over time, can wear you out. You can be tired of that tuna casserole you have every week or those weeds in your yard that come back again and again.
3. You can also more generally be tired of being tired. Do you ever wish you were more energetic? Social? Patient? Kind? As we saw in this chapter, your first- and second-order desires can be a struggle to bring into harmony.
4. This essay suggests turning to the right persons at the right times can be valuable in dealing with our inner turmoil. Do you know who to turn to and when?
5. Are you comfortable letting other people care for you, even if you can't reciprocate? Would that undermine your sense of yourself as strong? As competent? As independent? As reliable? Do you prefer to be the helper rather than the helped? Why?
6. Do you ever give of yourself without expecting anything in return? If not, would you like to do so?

3

Our Relationship with Others

An Empathetic Heart

> "If we could read the secret history of our enemies, we should find in each man's life sorrow and suffering enough to disarm all hostility."
>
> Henry Wadsworth Longfellow

Discovering Your Social Self

From Integrity to Empathy

In developing the virtue of an empathetic heart, you come to recognize yourself as a social creature. For at the core of this virtue is the capacity to put yourself in another person's place.

Thus, while a holistic mind aims for a clarity of thought, an empathetic heart aspires to a more fundamental deepening of your emotional capacity. It is primarily through developing your emotional sympathies that you can come to understand and respond appropriately to the thoughts, feelings, and experiences of others through an imaginative or sympathetic participation in their lives.

The virtue of an empathetic heart exposes the limits of a "stand alone" integrity. To be sure, before you can put yourself in another's place, you must first be a self. But as social creatures, a coherent and integrated, yet solitary, self is incomplete. You might say just as integrity is an essential ground for developing empathy, so empathy is necessary for the full maturation of integrity. This too will be part of the story you wish to tell about yourself.

Empathy plays this role for integrity's maturation because of integrity's third element. Integrity, you will recall, requires character, a coherence informed by ethical values. Because of the way empathy fosters your emotional sympathies for others, it helps to insure there is a critical moral center to your integrity.

Seeking your Better Self: Timely Virtues for a Turbulent World, First Edition. Jeffrey Nesteruk.
© 2026 John Wiley & Sons, Inc. All rights reserved, including rights for text and data mining and training of artificial intelligence technologies or similar technologies. Published 2026 by John Wiley & Sons, Inc.

Evading the Ego Trap

Our implicit egoism is something a number of psychological studies have confirmed. In many respects, this is not surprising. For implicit egoism is simply our tendency to favor or feel positively about things we associate with ourselves. As David G. Myers states, "For example, we come to like familiar things, including our own familiar face. Thus, we prefer a politician or stranger who looks like us ...."

But as Myers points out, this tendency goes further than many of us might suspect. He notes, for instance, the "name-letter effect." "People," he writes, "of varied nationalities, languages, and ages prefer letters that appear in their own name. People also tend to marry someone whose first or last name resembles their own."

I've had to catch this tendency in myself when I've been involved in hiring new professors. Degrees from liberal arts colleges or large research universities like the ones I attended immediately catch my eye whenever I come across them on a candidate's application. I've had to train myself to give such degrees their due, but not let my positive associations cloud my judgment.

And I've certainly experienced this kind of familiarity when I've been job hunting myself. I recall getting a favorable greeting when my bearded interviewer noted my own facial hair, unusual at the time in his office. I remember too a department chair complimenting me on my scholarly presentation, noting that my New England accent reminded him of his wife's. In both cases, I received job offers – ones that I hope were deserved. But I'm sure such familiar markers didn't hurt my chances.

As my classes regularly cover controversial ethical issues, I often find myself in the midst of passionate exchanges among my students. Indeed, I encourage such exchanges yet tend to keep my own views out of the fray. As I tell students, my job is not to tell you what to think but to help you learn how to think for yourselves. I studiously wish to avoid students parroting my views, thinking it may help them get a better grade. Like the rest of us, students are well aware of the benefits familiarity may bestow, even unconsciously.

An Undercurrent of Loneliness

While psychologists regularly tell us that a rich and varied social life is a key element in our well-being, it's hard to avoid the impression that as of late, we're not very good at it.

You don't have to spend much time on a college campus nowadays before you realize how much students are struggling. Not that I didn't struggle a generation ago during my college years. But student struggles today feel different. Their mental health is part and parcel of campus culture. Studies regularly report significant levels of anxiety and depression, even suicidal ideation. And stress seems an intimate and pervasive part of their lives, far more prominent than I recall as a student. As a professor, I find myself listening to students sharing stories of psychological counseling and prescriptions for therapeutic drugs. They talk more openly and intimately with me than I did with my professors. So many of them seem to be looking for someone who is willing to spend some time listening to them. I've learned to welcome their sharing of their wobbly moments.

Through these exchanges, I've been practicing my stumbling development of the virtue of an empathetic heart. It's worth the effort.

Over my years of teaching, I've found it's important to listen carefully to student conversations, considering the clues their words convey about future directions of our larger society. They will, after all, be the teachers of tomorrow. One of the most emotionally powerful aspects of being a teacher is that by paying attention to your students, you can glimpse the world to come.

Unfortunately, one of the things I see more of is an undercurrent of loneliness. It's not always what's on top, displayed in the surface content of their words, but it's there as an unsettling presence.

Complicating matters too, they are about to enter into a society in which our inability to form deep and satisfying connections with others is increasingly pervasive. During his tenure, United States Surgeon General Dr. Vivek Murthy released a Surgeon General Advisory characterizing loneliness as a public health crisis, saying its contribution to premature deaths is comparable to that of smoking daily.

Our Precarious Common World

Our inability to form more daily connections with each other is particularly troublesome when it comes to engaging with others different from ourselves. Here we can often think we are connecting when in fact we are not. The message we intend can vary widely from the message received. As George Bernard Shaw noted, "The greatest problem in communication is the illusion that it has been accomplished."

This is exacerbated by the splintering of our media and our abilities on the internet to hide in the echo chambers of like-minded folks. In the current political climate, I have difficulty seeing a common world that individuals of varying political stripes recognize and inhabit together. As social creatures, we are increasingly inhabiting different, frequently incommensurable, realities. Even family holiday dinners are getting difficult.

At the same time, we are reluctant to admit of different points of view as we pursue our daily endeavors. We like to think there is only one reality – and *it* is ours. Folks who see things differently are misguided or confused or, even perhaps, possessive of malevolent intentions. Framing our relationships in this way, we are likely to agree with philosopher Jean Paul Sartre's declaration that "Hell is other people."

Particularly in the intimacy of potential romantic partners, we are leery of difference, expecting a mathematical match of aims and desires. One of my favorite lines from a long-ago MASH episode reflects the complaints I hear from my friends on the online dating apps. Hawkeye tells Margaret, "We're both looking for a custom fit in an off-the-rack world."

But all of this is missing something essential about the nature of ourselves as social beings. I recall a minister once said to me of marriage, "If both of you are exactly the same, one of you is redundant." Given the psychological lures of implicit egoism, this is a point worth pursuing. For in expecting to be unchanged by our relationships, we are going about our relationships in precisely the wrong way.

Transformational Communities

The virtue of an empathetic heart runs deeper than is immediately apparent. This is because it calls for more than devoting additional time to our relationships or expanding the number of relationships we have. Rather, it aims for a fundamentally different understanding of the relationships themselves. Developing our capacities for empathy, especially for those who differ from us, opens up the possibility for relationships of a distinctive character – relationships that are less transactional and more transformational.

Consider, for a moment, your notion of "society." What comes to mind when you try to think more about this abstract concept and bring it into focus? Are your associations positive or negative? If you look beyond the people you know well, what of the rest you know indirectly or not at all? What assumptions do you make about their characters, needs, hopes, or aspirations? We all have tacit and often unreflected-upon assumptions about our fellow community members. It is worth trying to bring these unexamined assumptions to light.

It is easy today to unwittingly develop an atomistic view of community. As individuals, we can see ourselves as separate and autonomous. Indeed, this independent existence is something we frequently strive for and celebrate. As such, our relationships have an external, contingent character. We enter into them to meet our needs and achieve our goals, but in the process, expect the self we bring to these relationships to persist. We transact with each other, each of us getting something we want, but together miss the transformative possibilities of a deepening of our relationship.

Philosopher Robert Solomon lays out an alternative vision of community, one that is central to the development of the virtue of an empathetic heart. "What it means to be part of a community," he writes, "is something more than cooperation, something more than having something ('a commons') in common. It is, among other things, to identify yourself and your interests in and with the community. It is, simply, to become a different person."

This is what is ultimately at stake in the relationships we pursue. Not merely the needs we meet or the goals we achieve, but the persons we become. The deep and satisfying relationships we crave, even when we fail to acknowledge or resist them, are those in which a new and better version of ourselves emerges and develops. "It is not from ourselves," writes the poet Wendell Berry, "that we learn to be better than we are."

This is a piece of ancient wisdom. Good people, Aristotle emphasized, require a good community. Aristotelean scholar Edwin Hartman explains, "But for a good person, in particular a cooperator inclined to trust others, life in a community full of treacherous free riders would be unhappy. So we can see the point of Aristotle's claim that a virtuous person must live in a great *polis* – can only survive in a good community, we might say."

If seeking our better selves requires finding and entering into good communities, our task is a daunting one. For communities we encounter today are often enfeebled ones, if evaluated by this higher standard of promoting the positive development of those who inhabit them. With the distinctly modern precarity of a common world, we often don't even meet Solomon's minimal requirement of "having something ('a commons') in common."

So, how to begin? How do we develop relationships that are not merely enabling but ennobling? Relationships through which we better ourselves by bettering the lives of others.

This is the fundamental work of developing an empathetic heart. Crucially, it's not a step that you can take alone.

As it's not a step you can take alone, it will depend on you developing your empathy for others. As we extend our empathy most easily to those with whom we are most familiar, we might fruitfully begin by reflecting upon friendship.

Friendship

Reflecting upon Friendship

Certainly, when we reflect upon the nature of friendship, there is much to consider. As a popular phenomenon, friendship is freighted with multiple, sometimes contradictory, meanings and associations. From the classic TV sitcom, *Friends*, to the emergence of bromance among male suitors on the latest *Golden Bachelorette* reality show, the search for friendship is a broad and compelling part of our lives.

Coupled with this emotional need is the often strategically cruel use of its opposite. One of the most painful experiences for teenagers is exclusion from a favored group of peers. This can range from rejection at a lunch table to hallway taunts that "No one likes you" to online bullying with results as serious as suicide by a beleaguered youngster. To be sure, this sort of behavior is hardly absent from their adult counterparts. I recall a colleague at another university complaining to me about how much the social dynamics of the faculty dining room reminded him of the pettiness and immaturity of his junior high school cafeteria.

Simply getting a handle on what we mean when we speak of friendship can be a challenge. Consulting an online dictionary for the meaning of "friend," one finds everything from "a person whom one knows and with whom one has a bond of mutual affection, typically exclusive of sexual or family relations" to "a supporter of a cause, organization, or country by giving financial or other help" to simply someone "who is not an enemy or who is on the same side." A friend can even be something other than a person, simply "a familiar or helpful thing" like a memorable book. And, of course, with the constant connectivity of our online world, a friend can be someone physically absent from your life, "a contact associated with a social networking website."

The classic philosophical discussion of friendship comes from Aristotle. It's been surprising to me – in a deeply pleasurable way – to see how much Aristotle's insights resonate with my college students today. Most are unacquainted with what he had to say on the topic. Some of them even know little about him beyond his name. But bring his thoughts into an office hour conversation, and they immediately get what he means – and often want to know more.

Let's take a look at what he had to say.

Three Types of Friendship

Aristotle saw friendship as spanning three broad categories. He discussed friendship based on pleasure, friendship based on utility, and friendship based on virtue or a person's character. All are good, but appreciating the nature of each is important for a fully flourishing life. In developing each, I'd add, empathy helps to pave the way. For true friendship of any kind requires entering into the experience of another. As friendships depend on pleasure, utility, and virtue, they require an appreciation of other persons' wants, needs, and aspirations.

Friendship Based on Pleasure

This form of friendship is one my students and the rest of us easily recognize. If there is one core aspect of how we understand friendship, it's that it is founded on those whose relationships bring us pleasure. One of the central reasons we seek out our friends is that they are fun to be around. Friends are folks with whom we like "hanging out," as my students say. With our friends, we experience an array of positive emotions, such as affection, joy, and a sense of belonging, comfort, and safety. And as those who wish to foster our engagement with social media well know, we can come to crave the dopamine hit that accompanies a friendly response to our online posting in the form of a like, a thumbs up emoji, or a smiley face.

With the pleasure our friends bring to our lives, we commonly regard friendship as an important, even essential, part of a good life. In bringing our whole selves to an undertaking of moral development, this makes eminent sense. For, as we emphasized in the introductory chapter, the good life has a dual sense: It is good in the sense of something we admire and good in the sense of something we desire. And pleasure in its various forms is something we certainly desire. Indeed, it can be something that we overly desire, pursuing our selfish pleasures without regard to their consequences or the needs of others.

Thus, failing to incorporate our sense of what is admirable into our friendships clearly has ethical drawbacks. But the deleterious consequences extend beyond those of moral turpitude. Recall the ever-present psychological dynamic of the hedonic treadmill, where you need increasingly higher achievements to maintain a baseline of satisfaction. If your first social media posting gets a hundred likes, your second posting will have to do better or else it will be a disappointment. And there are simply practical limits to seeking pleasure in a merely additive manner. As I heard one Hollywood movie star recount, you can't have a hundred best friends.

Of course, Aristotle was well aware of the limits of hedonistic lifestyles. His understanding of friendship included our need for utility in our relationships.

Friendship Based on Utility

Our friends do much more than enrich our lives through enjoyable experiences. Our friends have a broader utility. They can be the ones that take class notes for us when we're sick, provide references for that new job we're seeking, and offer to take us to the grocery store when we're no longer able to drive ourselves. In short, friends are useful. They can give us a helping hand to get through the difficult times and a push forward when we're seeking new opportunities.

My students readily identify with the usefulness of friends when they are seeking an internship or that first job out of college. Indeed, networking is second nature for them in ways that go beyond my less worldly mindset during my student days. Colleges and universities are offering greater support and guidance here. Available are a plethora of new online resources, such as the popular Handshake.

But my students are also aware of the consequences of adopting a purely utilitarian attitude toward relationships. No one wants to be "used," whether it's being taken advantage of in a weekend "hook-up" or in shouldering a disproportionate amount of work for a group class assignment. An adherence to utility loses its ethical shine when the use at issue isn't offered voluntarily or fails to respect the welfare of the one providing it.

Yet there is still a strongly positive connotation to utility in the relationships we seek. Everyone wants, in some sense, to be useful. It is one of the ways we affirm our dignity and value. Many of my retired friends volunteer, working at a soup kitchen, tutoring a GED class, or providing pro bono legal advice.

And as we experience often-diminishing capacities as we get older, we fear no longer being of use. We as a society should be more careful with the stereotypes we fall into in this regard. I recall my mother in her nineties wisely saying, "Well, you can always pray," and her prayers were something I was always grateful for.

Thus, utility is something of an ethical mixed bag. Much depends on how we understand it and when and how we employ it. But Aristotle saw a third type of friendship that, for him, was, in many ways, the most significant one.

Friendship Based on Virtue
For Aristotle, the ultimate form of friendship arises not out of pleasure or utility. It does not depend on you finding another person's companionship enjoyable or that person's ability or position to be of instrumental value to you. It depends not on what the other person could do for you, but more fundamentally, on who that person is. It depends on that person's character. And for Aristotle, character has a profound ethical sense.

While this may not be the most immediate way we tend to think about friendship, it's still an abiding presence in the friendships we value most. If you think for a moment of your best friend, you will likely see qualities in this person you admire. He might be someone who keeps his promises to you. She might be someone who treats others kindly. He might be someone who is steadfast in challenging situations. She might be someone you know you can depend on to tell you the truth, even when you don't want to hear it.

These are the friendships that, as Aristotle recognized, are the ones that are most permanent and enduring. They are the friendships you can count on, even as your life evolves and situations change. For what you found pleasurable as a teenager is likely to have changed as you contemplate your retirement. The coffee I'd never touch growing up now is an anticipated pleasure with my leisurely morning breakfast. And what is of use to you alters at each life stage. With all my academic degrees behind me, I'm long past the need for recommendations for admission to graduate school programs.

Equally important is the added dimension this third type of friendship brings to an undertaking of personal moral development. Unless we mindfully attend to them, friendships of pleasure and utility can at times slip easily into transactional exchanges. They are relationships in which you receive something, for example, a social outing you enjoy or a tip on a job opening you need, but your character remains fundamentally unchanged in the process. In contrast, friendships based on virtue intrinsically tend toward the transformational. An enduring interaction and evolving closeness with someone you admire over time seldom leaves you where you started. You are likely to learn things, ask probing questions, and conceive of who you want to be anew.

And therein ultimately lies the value of the virtue of an empathetic heart.

Working Toward an Empathetic Heart

In the opening quote for this chapter, the poet Henry Wadsworth Longfellow speaks of the "secret history" of others. In doing so, he captures the essential challenge in developing the virtue of an empathetic heart. At the root of the challenge is the recognition of how much the interior life of others, even those who are part of our everyday routines, is a secret history, kept from daily view. It is easy to miss this "sorrow and suffering" as we get caught up in the stresses and practical demands of our own lives. After all, what I want from my coworker is to get a timely response to my urgent email, not to hear about the illness of his mother. At the deli counter, I'm looking to receive some thinly sliced turkey breast, not hear the concern of the fellow behind the counter about his recent discovery of his daughter's hidden drug use. But Longfellow insists these secret histories run deep, profound enough that should we learn of them, they would "disarm all hostility," even toward our enemies.

In fostering such deeper awareness of the trials of others, an empathetic heart is a key to the transformational potential of relationships, even with those who irritate or frustrate us. The more we can sympathetically and imaginatively enter into the painful experience of others, the more we can recast the hardened postures they present to us. The impatient customer may have been up last night dealing with a sick child. The plumber who's late to repair your leaking faucet may just have received bad news about his latest medical test. The relative who's never on time for a family dinner may not like the way your spouse treats him.

Along with helping us recast our troublesome relationships, an empathetic heart can move you forward in positive ways. We've all heard the advice that you should dress not for the position you currently have, but for the position you hope to obtain. In a similar fashion, you may choose aspirational relationships, those that don't simply reinforce your current makeup but that foster the person you want to be.

I try to spend time with individuals who bring out the best in me, like my grandfather when I was young. Unlike my frequent use of the microwave, he would patiently spend over an hour making a salad for dinner, but they were the best salads I've ever tasted. Whenever I'm losing my patience, which happens more than I'd like, I think of what he accomplished in his long life going slow and steady. If you look around in your own life, I'm sure you'll find equivalent examples too. Could be a spouse. Could be a friend. Could be the school crosswalk guard shepherding those rambunctious kindergarteners across the street. As you invest in attending to the inner life of others, you will discover glimpses of inspiration all around you.

Beyond Friendship: From the Familiar to the Far-off

Extending Your Empathy

Up until now, we've mainly looked at developing an empathetic heart in your more immediate surroundings. We've mentioned spouses and children, coworkers and shopkeepers, and the kind of folks with whom you have more intimate relations or face-to-face encounters. In such embodied and concrete contexts, our moral intuitions are more readily activated. Simply look at how we are so evolutionarily responsive to the crying of infants!

But there are clear limits to how many socially rich relationships we can have. Anthropologist Robin Dunbar argued that human beings can only maintain these kinds of stable social relationships up to groups of about 150 persons, a figure now known as Dunbar's number. Beyond that, there is a cognitive overload with handling the kind of informational input required to monitor and maintain these relationships.

Of course, the technologically connected world we now live in vastly expands our possible contacts and connections. We quickly learn of everything from earthquakes to missile attacks to virus outbreaks from around the world, even observing such events in real time.

Developing empathy involves understanding its advantages and extending their reach. Properly fostered, it can apply not only to the familiar – close relationships rich with daily interactions – but also to the far-off – relationships with distant individuals, whether the distance arises from geography, culture, or life experience.

Our relationships with this larger set of human experiences, however, have a different character than a crying child at our feet. Entering sympathetically and imaginatively into the experiences of those we encounter in these more abstract or attenuated ways represents a different kind of challenge. How do we go about extending our empathy from the familiar to the far-off? In aiming to overcome the psychological dynamic of implicit egoism here, we need to call upon an additional set of moral skills.

It's thus time to take a deeper look at ethical theory. It's a step you need to take if you want to raise your sights and tell a larger story about yourself.

A Dip into Ethical Theory

In a fundamental way, we are not built for the world we currently inhabit. When it comes to engaging our moral intuitions and sympathies, our immediate environments have a disproportionate role. Our evolutionary development prepared us to make choices within concrete social and physical environments. Not surprisingly, our moral sense followed suit. Our empathy is more readily engaged by any suffering or stress we have before our eyes.

It's not that we are incapable of having a larger angle of ethical vision that extends beyond our immediate experience. But here, we can benefit from the help of employing specific strategies.

For example, good literature can extend our awareness and engagement with the interior lives of others, even those far removed by geography, culture, or life experience. There is a reason we can all still be moved by Shakespeare's Hamlet or Plato's Republic.

Well-crafted and existentially rich stories bringing us into the lives of others – particularly their interior lives – are a necessary counterpoint to our naturally self-oriented tendencies. They help to foster the expansion of a healthy and well-balanced empathy.

Surveys, as we noted earlier, show that most individuals view themselves as ethically above average, something that is mathematically suspect. One reason this occurs is that while we know our interior world and external actions, others for the most part know only our external actions. Thus, because others lack ready access to our reasons that may cast our actions in a different light, they are inclined toward harsher judgements of our choices. To the degree we can employ strategies to help us see the world from the perspectives of others, we can help our innate sense of empathy reach its full potential and development.

This is where ethical theory has an important role to play. It too can be employed as a strategy to extend and develop our empathetic sensibilities. It can help us look beyond ourselves in new ways.

An Example to Get You Started

Ponder for a moment the following question: Would you cut off one of your fingers to save the lives of 10 anonymous individuals you would never know or meet?

This example, which I've shared many times with students and others, tends to get some awkward or unsettled reactions. Even as a hypothetical, it can prompt a wobbly moment or two. Some folks tend to scoff a bit, saying dismissively that it's not a realistic situation. This, of course, is true. It's certainly not something we'd face as part of our daily routines. Indeed, most likely, it's something we would never encounter.

But note the implied need lurking behind this common dismissive reaction. Individuals have this dismissive reaction because they are looking for a more realistic situation in which to exercise their ethical judgement. They want a way of situating their ethical choice within a context that is more familiar to them.

They want to place this decision in the world of their more immediate experience. Without saying so, they are demonstrating the way our moral intuitions work – they are at their best within a familiar experiential framework. This is confirmed by the way students often press me for more context with this example before making an ethical choice.

Would your ethical sense of this finger-cutting choice shift if these anonymous individuals were aware that you made this choice to save their lives? Would your ethical calculus alter in any way if these individuals knew you were even offered such a choice? Would you have to fundamentally recalibrate your choice if you knew these ten individuals? What if these ten individuals consisted of close family and friends?

Wherever your moral intuitions led you in contemplating these questions, pay careful attention to any revisions in your choices that occurred as I offered differing contexts. It is these moral intuitions that ethical theory is designed to develop.

Three Ethical Theories

Ethical theories aim at giving a more conceptual elaboration of our moral intuitions. As such, they can clarify and extend for us our understanding of everyday moral responses.

We are drawing upon ethical theory here to explore how it can broaden our focus and extend our empathy. It is thus a fundamental part of the development of the virtue of an empathetic heart. It is the next step in the virtue's undertaking of socializing yourself and thus reenvisioning your relationships with others.

For our purposes, we will be dealing with only the general import of three theories of ethics, leaving aside many finer distinctions. For instance, we will for the moment overlook Bentham's idea of the good as simply a ratio of pleasure and pain. In sketching with a broad brush here, I want to focus in a general way on how you can draw upon ethical theory to enhance and enrich your moral intuitions. Our aim here is a focus on practical use, not theoretical precision.

Like many ethicists today, I have, during my career, been engaged by three central ethical theories, or as I prefer to call them following Robert Solomon, ethical styles. These three forms of ethical thinking are virtue ethics, deontological ethics, and utilitarian ethics. Prominent representatives of each theory are, respectively, Aristotle, Immanuel Kant, and Jeremy Bentham. Each of these three ethical approaches has, in its own way, been deeply influential within Western thought, and at certain points, well beyond.

While there can be much overlap in their analyses, their divergence occurs because of their fundamentally different orientations. Aristotle's approach centers on a person's character, Kant's on a person's actions, and Bentham's on the consequences of a person's actions.

Of course, in the dynamic richness of human experience, we can't sharply isolate each of these three elements from the others. It's hard to think clearly about a person's character without an awareness of his actions and even harder to think with perspicuity about a person's actions without acknowledging their consequences.

The contribution of the relationship-based model of ethics in *Seeking Your Better Self* is the way it performs an integrative function here. For the kind of relationships we regard as worth striving for, the kind we're willing to invest our time and energy in, require an admirable excellence across the entirety of a person, his actions, and their consequences. Framing ethics around the quality of relationships is ethics as-lived, not ethics as-theorized-about. It can thus bring the illuminations of theory to our daily lives in a way that encourages our personal investment and moral growth.

Let's take a look at each of these three ethical theories in turn to see what we might learn.

Bentham on the Consequences of a Person's Actions
In our daily routines and encounters, our moral intuitions often reflect concerns about the consequences of our actions. Even young children will hesitate to hit a sibling in the midst of a dispute out of a fear of a parent's punishment. This is also true in the everyday actions of our lives as adults. We stop at red lights, knowing the potentially dangerous consequences of failing to do so. And even when the traffic looks clear, we know that speeding through a light that just turned red may attract the attention of a nearby police officer. Nowadays, punishment may follow even without the presence of human authority. I learned my lesson well recently when an automatic camera snapped a picture of me going through a just-turned red light. It will be interesting to see how the wider adoption of such camera technology will alter the evolution of our moral intuitions. But for now, I just had to pay a $75 fine that arrived through the mail.

But as these examples show, in considering the consequences of our actions, we most immediately consider the consequences that directly affect ourselves. In Bentham's utilitarianism, the moral calculus is expanded. Ethical decision-making requires a consideration of all the consequences, both good and bad and, crucially, to ourselves *and* others. For Bentham, this is an essential step in socializing ourselves.

With this step, Bentham insists on an expansion of our moral sympathies. At least in a rudimentary way, we have to consider the effects of our actions upon others. In checking our immediate selfish impulses, we need to reframe our relationships with other persons, opening the door for an expansion of our empathy. This is because a full consideration of the effects of our actions upon another person requires some understanding of that other person's welfare, his thoughts and feelings, and his experience of the world. This can help to foster our capacity to imaginatively and sympathetically put ourselves in this other person's place.

Without this kind of empathy for other persons, our ethical calculations can easily get out-of-whack. This is going to be a key issue, for instance, in the programming of self-driving cars. Consider a situation in which such a self-driving car has to choose between injuring its driver and injuring a pedestrian crossing the street. How should the designers of this car program it to make such a choice? The choice involves taking account of the welfare of the pedestrian along with that of the driver. Without any sort of empathy for the pedestrian, the designer's choice would obviously be morally flawed. Yet as a buyer and likely driver of a car, which programmed car would you choose to purchase? Without developing empathy, you might think only of your own safety, thus choosing one that prioritized the driver. But that might not be a socially optimal result. This may well be a case in which regulation is required if we take seriously Bentham's injunction that ethical choices require the consideration of all the consequences.

Enlarging our utilitarian calculus as Bentham's theory calls for is a helpful step forward, aiding the development of the virtue of an empathetic heart. But this utilitarian calculus misses our more everyday moral intuitions in two important respects.

To begin with, we tend to exhibit greater concern and thus feel a greater obligation toward those people we are closest to. In particular, this intuition comes to the fore when we consider close family relations, such as spouses and children. A classic philosophical example that tests Bentham's utilitarian approach: You are on a dock overlooking the water. On one side, your daughter is drowning. On the other side, Albert Einstein is drowning. You only have time to save one of them. Which one would you choose? Without going further into innumerable possible details, if we stipulate Einstein's entire life's work produced more good for the world than your daughter's life efforts, the answer from a utilitarian perspective is clear: You save Einstein. But that is hardly where the intuition of a loving parent is likely to be.

Secondly, Bentham's ethical theory seems to miss something of our ethical intuitions regarding our obligations that arise out of past actions. Consider another classic philosophical scenario: Suppose you and your friend are lost in the desert wilderness with the supply of water running low. Calculating the days it will take you both to reach safety, you realize your water supply will run out beforehand. So, your friend makes you a deal. He has a million dollars in a secret account. He says if you promise to give that million dollars to his girlfriend should you survive and reach safety, he will let you have all the water, relinquishing his half. You promise to do so and make it back safely, but unfortunately, he does not.

You intend to give the million dollars to his girlfriend, but after doing some investigation, you learn she is already a wealthy billionaire. You know too that your mother-in-law needs an expensive operation that this million could fund. The million dollars is of a relatively less benefit to the billionaire girlfriend than is the lifesaving benefit to your mother-in-law. What would you do? Bentham's utilitarian analysis would favor giving the money to your mother-in-law, though our moral intuitions generally guide us to take account not only of future consequences but past obligations.

A form of Bentham's utilitarian approach is very much in the news nowadays, under the banner of "effective altruism." It has gained a particular prominence among those in the finance and high technology industries, notably championed by Sam Bankman-Fried, former CEO of FTX, before the collapse of his company and subsequent sentencing. The idea is to spend your early years amassing tremendous wealth and then giving much of it away to promote the social good.

The effective altruism movement is a good example of utilitarianism's forward-looking character. With its emphasis on consequences, it is inherently future-oriented, marginalizing obligations arising out of our past actions. Particularly among effective altruism advocates, there is also a strand of depersonalization in its forward-looking calculus of utility. As persons, we tend to feel a greater ethical obligation to those closest to us. For effective altruism advocates, this is a form of questionable favoritism, which doesn't pass muster under clear and rigorous analysis.

Kant on a Person's Action

For Kant, our ethical focus shouldn't be simply on consequences, on what follows after an action, but on the action itself. The ethical quality of an action is evident in the very nature of the action. Some actions are right, some actions are wrong, irrespective of their consequences.

The ethical quality of an individual's action is subject to a test Kant provides, one he refers to as the categorical imperative. Under one of its formulations: "Act only according to that maxim whereby you can at the same time will that it should become a universal law." While put in this technical manner, it simply means we should act upon rules that apply to everyone, regardless of their status or situation.

Thus, for example, we should keep our promises because we can't without contradiction will that others break their promises to us. Kant's categorical imperative bears a striking similarity to The Golden Rule, expressed in different ways in many of the world's major religions. As a maxim, "Do unto others as you wish them to do unto you" draws upon the same widely shared moral intuition that we should accord others the same respect and consideration we more readily give to ourselves.

Thus, Kant's categorical imperative can be drawn upon to expand our ethical sympathies, enlarging our empathetic sentiments. While Bentham brings the welfare of other persons to the fore through his emphasis on the consequences of our actions, Kant highlights the needs of others by directing our attention to our own deeply felt concerns. We too want others to keep their promises to us. Both theories provide a check on our implicit egoism, helping to reorient our focus on self to be more inclusive of others.

Like Bentham, Kant extends our moral sympathies beyond our immediate engagements and context by insisting on universalizing the moral principles that should guide our choices. To the degree we can, through our efforts over time, incorporate these more abstract principles into our daily habits and practices, we can extend our moral sympathies and more fully develop the virtue of an empathetic heart.

In terms of developing an empathetic heart, Kant's approach excels at providing a check on our natural tendency to view our own situations and choices as exceptional in some way, as involving some acceptable deviation from what otherwise would be the general rule. The student who never would cheat except "this teacher's tests are unfair." The neighbor who always picks up his dog's poop "but I'm late for a business meeting today." The parent who would never hit his child "but nothing else seems to stop him from mouthing off." Kant's approach does so because it compels us to consider whether we would accept such deviations if we bore the brunt of them.

And yet: There are times when rules rigidly applied miss their moral mark, disrupting a more appropriately empathetic response. In this regard, Aristotle has something to say about how rules fail to capture the nuances of life's moral challenges.

Aristotle on a Person's Character

Aristotle wants to redirect our primary ethical focus. His central concern is not a person's actions or their consequences, as we saw with Kant and Bentham, but rather a person's character. This is because it is an individual's character – his basic underlying traits or dispositions – that gives rise to his actions and their consequences. For Aristotle, our moral development consists of actions developing into habits that evolve into character. As he famously said, a person becomes just by doing just actions.

This sort of dynamic of expected moral development is one that is readily familiar to parents and children. If your child were to steal something, you might reprimand him, making him return the item with an apology. But our hope as parents is that by encouraging actions that respect another's property, this kind of respect develops into a habit that becomes second nature, even when punishment is no longer present or can be avoided. We want this respect for the property of others to become part of our child's basic disposition and orientation as he matures into adulthood.

Along with the theories of Bentham and Kant, this type of ethical thinking can play a role in developing and extending our empathy toward others. For if the source of our actions is our character, rooted in our underlying traits or dispositions, this basic orientation has an enduring quality. Thus, if we desire to extend the reach of our empathy, Aristotle points our attention to our core nature. Our core nature, as was our focus in Chapter 2, shouldn't vary casually from setting to setting or in the face of difficult circumstances. With this as the source of our empathy, we can gain an empathetic heart that transcends our immediate surroundings.

Aristotle's thinking about ethics thus suggests we look beyond the kind of rules that Bentham and Kant espouse to role models for developing our moral sentiments and sympathies. When I look around at parents, friends, and colleagues, I find plenty who exhibit specific moral qualities in greater measure than I do. It isn't hard for me to find among those in my life someone who is kinder, more courageous, or more regularly self-sacrificing than I am. I suspect I am not alone in this regard. Taking our cue from Aristotle, we can turn to the more empathetic among us. In our wobbly moments, we can bring to mind those whose character exhibits the empathy we strive for. At the very least, bringing such individuals to mind provides a touchstone to engage as we make our own choices.

***

In Chapter 2, we emphasized the importance of developing a coherent conception of self and aspiring to integrity. But while this is an essential part of any undertaking of moral growth, it falls short if it proceeds in isolation.

This is because for better or worse – and as you can now see, I think on the whole it is for better – we are social creatures. Thus, the relationships in which your life is embedded are an integral part of who you are.

By developing the virtue of an empathetic heart, you are able to tap into the positive transformational possibilities your interactions with other persons offer you. For by entering imaginatively and sympathetically into the experiences of others, you can gain new perspectives and insights not available to you within the strictures of your own outlook. As the poet Wendell Berry reminded us, "It is not from ourselves that we learn to be better than we are."

Topical Reflections

Just as was true of our relationship with ourselves, thinking broadly about our relationship to others can only take us so far. Let's now take a closer look at the way the ethical challenges and opportunities of our connections with others surface in our daily experiences. As before, the topical reflections draw upon experiences that are my own, yet by engaging the questions that follow, I hope you can find insights that are uniquely yours.

***

Friendship is one of the central themes of this chapter. In the following essay, you will meet my friend, Janine. I've known her for over forty years. I wish for all of you a friend like Janine.

Friends

I used to say: Janine is my oldest friend. But she doesn't let me say that anymore. Now that she has edged past 40, she doesn't like the ambiguity of "oldest" even when coupled with "friend." So, now I say: She's my friend of longest duration.

We met in college. At dinner one evening, she reached over to my plate to sample some of the food upon it. Strangers at the time, I thought her gesture an aggressive bit of intimacy. But it led to a comment and then a conversation. And that first conversation led to others.

It seems like we've been talking ever since.

It seems so even though we now live in different states and often go a stretch without seeing each other. As old friends, we enjoy the luxury of conversing in the perennial present. Each conversation begins as if there were no gap before it.

Most of our conversations occur with an electronic device in hand. The phone has become the mark and medium of our friendship.

But even the latest smart phone provides a strange kind of intimacy. It brings close the person's voice yet draws attention to the lack of physical proximity. It can remind you of how far away you are.

My over-the-phone friendship with Janine reveals the kind of temptations to which many of us have succumbed. We are more connected than ever before – by iPhones or iPads, from Twitter (now X) to texts. But our new ways of being connected mask a deeper disconnection in our relationships. Told it less matters where we are; we are more often separated. Our mobile lives produce the paradox of being physically distant from those closest to us.

In this regard, I am certainly one of the worst offenders. Early in my career, I moved five times in five years. Offered a series of increasingly better jobs, I had a freedom I couldn't resist exercising.

And even while in one place, I was often thinking of another.

Increasingly, our work promotes a tenuous relation to the places we inhabit. Our jobs are often more linked to happenings in Los Angeles or Vancouver or London than the view we see from our windows. At night, we enter chat rooms. During the day, we ignore our neighbors.

Even during these nomadic years, I managed to keep calling Janine. It was then I learned she was tolerant of calls at inconvenient hours, able to listen even after having her sleep disturbed.

But there's a cost to often being elsewhere than the emotional locus of our lives. We need to touch those we love and see the results of the work we do. Distances we transverse electronically, we do not experience concretely – and it becomes easy to imagine the world as other than it is.

The same is true of those we are closest to if we meet them too often as disembodied voices or silent words produced for a computer screen. We can begin to see them as other than they are.

I love the Internet. I am fascinated by the technology even as I fumble to master all its possibilities. Still, I've never felt the urge to e-mail Janine. The anonymity of the Net is antithetical to our relationship. It allows you to become what you want rather than see who you are.

In a less-mobile era, Janine would have been the girl down the street. I would have pushed her on the playground and flirted with her in high school. I would have sat on her front steps watching her first child play in the yard. I would have run into her without even planning to do so.

But tonight, I am fumbling to find her newly changed number, hoping to give her a call. Perhaps we'll talk of the last time we were together – the day she was married almost two years ago. I remember how we laughed at her wedding, how our feet stuck to the floor when we danced, and how it suddenly felt like a college fraternity party all over again.

Personal Reflection Prompts
1. Do you have a best friend? If you reflect upon the nature of that friendship, what is its basis? Thinking over our discussion in this chapter, is it a friendship based on pleasure? On utility? On virtue? On all three or something else?
2. Think of some more of your friends. What are the ways those persons have changed you? Positively? Negatively? And reverse the question: How have you changed them? Is there anything you wish was part of these friendships but is not? What, if anything, are you prepared to do about it?
3. Did you ever have a friendship come to an end? Did it end suddenly or gradually over time? Do you wish you had done anything differently? Did both of you understand why the friendship ended? Were you each able to empathize with the other?
4. How have the new technologies in your life changed your friendships? Is it easier for you to connect online? Harder? Just different?
5. Does your use of social media make you feel less alone? More alone? More trusting? Less trusting? More confident? Less confident? Could you give up social media? Do you want to do so?

6. How does your participation in larger groups affect your friendships? Do all your friends get along? Did friendship with one person ever entail rejecting another person? How exclusive do you want your friendships to be? Have you ever been jealous of a friend's friendship with someone else? Are there friendships that work better not as pairs, but as threesomes, foursomes, fivesomes, and beyond? If you have a group chat, how much would you miss it?

***

This essay follows upon this chapter's emphasis on the transformative power of relationships. Such transformations can happen in ways that you might not expect or could easily miss, in moments as commonplace as conversations.

Conversation

I've been noticing lately: So much talk, so little good conversation.

Indeed, much of the talk in our lives doesn't even rise to the level of a conversation, good or otherwise. We often interact in ways that fall short of a genuine exchange. Father reprimands son. Salesperson pressures customer. Boss fires underling. Two people may be talking, but there is no conversation.

Underneath the talk is an often-unrecognized dilemma: not wanting conversation, but also not wanting silence. Conversation is difficult if you're uncomfortable with another. Silence is disconcerting if you're uncomfortable with yourself. So all over the country televisions are on in the background.

My friend David is someone I can count on for good conversations. At their best, they begin with dinner, go on through the evening, and end only in the early morning hours. David is brilliant, but more than his brilliance drives our late-night exchanges. It is his willingness to find some value in *everything* I say. Even when he thinks I'm wrong, he responds to my words in a way that develops their truth as well as reveals their error. Thus, around David, I feel like a more insightful person.

Indeed, I *am* a more insightful person. In a good conversation, the whole is always greater than the sum of the parts. This doesn't mean the parts can't stand alone. It only means that each in playing his role both preserves and transcends himself. In ways that are sometimes subtle, sometimes profound, each person becomes someone new.

The way I'm changed during my late-night exchanges with David reveals the essence of a good conversation. The core of a good conversation is more than the information it conveys, even more than the relationship it helps to create. Its fundamental value lies in who it allows each speaker to become.

Good conversations needn't have conclusions. Indeed, the best often don't. Rather than end, good conversations continue in some way even after they're over.

They open us up, start a new dynamic in motion. Something clouded becomes clear. Something new is funny. Something missed can now be seen.

Talk may be cheap, but good conversations are not. Good conversations require not only an investment of time and energy. They ask something more. Since good conversations can change people, they require the willingness to risk self-transformation.

We don't tend to place a high value on good conversation nowadays. We are a culture that wants to get things done. Good conversation seems to require time we don't have.

But while good conversations aren't overtly efficient, we shouldn't let their appearances deceive us. They are often the surest way to get us to where we need to be.

Rather than being divorced from action, good conversation is action of the most potent kind. Good conversations change people. They take you someplace you couldn't go alone. And the best conversations take you to your better self.

Whatever the task at hand, this is the person who can get the job done.

Good conversations needn't be lengthy or ponderous. Good conversation can occur even in the simplest of everyday exchanges. The best chit-chat has a sincerity to it even when it's filled with stock phrases ("Good morning. How are you? What's new?") This is because the sincerity arises not from the words but from the way of being such words intimate. It's a way of being that recognizes there's a humanity to relationships, even of the most cursory or commercial kind. It says, "I acknowledge you. You exist. You have an importance like me. And I want to respect you."

And even these brief exchanges sincerely engaged in can change the persons involved. At the very least, one now becomes someone who has acknowledged another, and the other becomes someone who has been acknowledged.

We can only value our conversations to the degree we realize what's at stake in them. Seeing our conversations as acts of self-creation elevates them to their proper station. It encourages us to seek them continually and attend to them properly.

Getting better at conversation entails first getting better at silence. This is because the mark of a good silence is self-comfort. And self-comfort is the key to the self-transformation of a good conversation. Only for a person comfortable with himself do the necessary risks become possible.

I'm going to begin by not leaving the television on in the background.

Personal Reflection Prompts

1. Are you a better person around some persons rather than others? Why do certain people bring out the best in you? Do you actively seek these people out? And what about you? Do you bring out the better qualities in others? Can you think of some examples? When this happens, why does this occur?

2. Reflect for a moment and consider the more memorable conversations you've had in your life. Pick out two or three that especially stand out for you. What made them memorable? Did you discover something important about yourself or the other person? Did you ever have a single conversation that led to a new direction in your life?
3. In this chapter, philosopher Robert Solomon asks what it means to be part of a community. He concludes, "It is, simply, to become a different person." Conversations between groups are certainly a form of community. Has your participation in conversational communities involved becoming a "different person"? Is there a difference between face-to-face communities and online communities? Have you ever left a community because it was making you "different"?
4. In your view, what's the key to have a good conversation? In this connection, how do you define "good"? What's the role of empathy in a good conversation?
5. Does familiarity help or hinder conversations? How can you best communicate with unfamiliar individuals or in unfamiliar settings? In this chapter George Bernard Shaw notes, "The greatest problem in communication is the illusion that it has been accomplished." Did you ever encounter such an illusion? How did you handle it?

***

The following essay explores one of the most powerful experiences empathy can engender – that of forgiveness.

Forgiveness

Forgiveness isn't much in vogue these days. It conflicts in basic ways with the I've-got-to-keep-one-step-ahead-of-the-next-guy spirit of our times. Forgiveness gives the other person a break, something we're not inclined to do, especially when the competition's keen.

But this perception misses a deeper truth about forgiveness. Forgiveness is an enormous good for the one forgiven, to be sure. But more fundamentally, forgiveness is a gift to the forgiver.

The trouble is it's a gift most of us aren't willing to accept.

The hardest part of forgiveness is not what is given to someone else, but rather what is accepted about yourself in performing such an act. You need to accept that you are no longer a person with a basis for anger, a reason for revenge, a justification for harm. You need to agree that fairness in the abstract will not, in this case, apply to you.

Forgiveness is nonetheless a gift because it offers a freedom that's otherwise unobtainable. The freedom it offers is a freedom from the harms that have been done to you.

In my student days, I had a passionate affair with a woman that ended in the worst possible way. She unable to talk about it. I unable to understand why. Hurt in a way I'd not been before, I was lost in the limbo of something finished yet never brought to a close.

So, struggling to get over her, I made up my own story, about how not my vices but my virtues were the root of our breakup, about how the things I stood for scared her away. The story let me be how I then needed to be – noble but numb.

But the story also hid an anger at her that wouldn't let me move on. I couldn't work, couldn't date, and couldn't think of much else. My anger bound me to her in a way our passion never had.

It bound me until a graceful moment, when something inside of me shifted, and I was able to forgive her. In that moment, my anger dissipated, and I could genuinely wish her well. For the first time in months, I was free.

When I wished her well, it wasn't everyday morality that had prevailed. Forgiveness isn't right or wrong in an ordinary sense. It's about not doing right when you have the right to do something wrong. It's about being better than part of you ever wants to be. It's a graceful moment.

We all have people we know we need to forgive. Our parents, our spouse, our children, and our siblings. Coworkers and contractors. The fellow who cut too sharply in front of us on the freeway yesterday.

We can even bear grudges without being aware of them. Some are buried deep. Some are too dangerous to acknowledge.

Feeling guilty or wishing to smooth over an uncomfortable conflict, we can feign forgiveness. But this misses the point. Forgiveness isn't like politeness. It's not something you can put on for show. With good manners, form can matter. With forgiveness, only substance does.

Feigning forgiveness is like pretending to breathe. Neither act gets you what you really need.

When we're hurting most, it's hardest to forgive. But even in these most difficult of times, there is a paradox to pain. The suffering that hardens us can also make us more empathetic.

Our suffering thus provides the possibility of a graceful moment. When the hurt we feel ceases to make us want to hurt others. When the pain instead fosters the resolve to keep others from pain.

It's this graceful moment that allows the possibility of forgiveness. When I see in the pain of another my own suffering, I see there's more to our relationship than the competition that often seems to consume it. There's also the responsibility that each has to limit the harm borne by the other.

There is, then, in forgiveness a reminder for me, as I strive to succeed in a get-ahead world. The reminder is of the deeper connection to others that underlies even the keenest competition. Remembering this deeper connection allows a larger notion of success. I want not only to be someone who gets ahead. I want to be someone who's ready to keep others from falling behind.

Personal Reflection Prompts

1. As you can gather from this essay, it can take me a long time to reach my "graceful moments." Truth be told, in regard to some parts of my life, I am wondering whether I'll ever get there. Have you ever had a graceful moment in which you were able to forgive another person? What enabled you to do it?
2. Henry Wadsworth Longfellow talks about the transforming effects of knowing the "secret history" of others. Have you ever shared a "secret history" of your own with another person? If you've ever done so, what happened? Reflecting back upon the romantic break-up during my student years, I realize that I never learned her secret history. How should you handle a relationship with someone who is unable or unwilling to share their secret history?
3. At the core of developing the virtue of an empathetic heart is expanding your capabilities for putting yourself in the place of another person. For those of which we know little or perhaps even nothing at all, can principles, such as those offered by ethical theory, help? What of the principle espoused at the end of this essay? Do you want to be not only someone who "gets ahead," but also someone "who's ready to keep others from falling behind"? As a practical matter, can you do both at the same time?
4. The essay states, "Forgiveness isn't right or wrong in an ordinary sense." Are there times when what is right as a general matter does not apply in a particular case? How do you recognize such a case? Remember too the cautions arising from our self-serving bias. We all can be overly generous with ourselves in thinking our particular situation is the exception. Have you ever given up something you had a right to do?

***

As this chapter emphasizes, we need to extend our empathy not only to those who are familiar but to those who are far-off. Distance comes in many ways and need not be physical. It can happen, as the following essay explores, across generations.

Sacrifice

I grew up thinking differently of sacrifice than did my father. Yet neither one of us is unusual. He is as typical of his generation as I am of mine.

You can see the difference in what he – and so many others his age – did not think about. He, for example, simply had the kids I first struggled over having.

My wife tells me how her dad worked two jobs in her youth. He'd come home from one for a quick dinner, then go out to the second, not returning until after midnight. He did this day in and day out. Yet ask him now how he managed it, and all you'll get is a shrug. He doesn't have an answer. He doesn't think one is necessary. He did what a man at that time with a family had to do.

As we go on in our marriage, my wife and I talk often of our parents, how much they sacrificed for us, yet how easy they made it look. Aware of our own struggles, this is for us the essence of the puzzle – the appearance of ease over what must have been difficult. It's as if there's something missing in ourselves that was part of our parents. Yet it's a part of themselves they couldn't fully recognize or explain.

Of course, the times have changed. Amid the looser roles of the new millennium, marriage – like so much of contemporary life – is more open-textured. So little determined, so much open to negotiation. We have more choices.

But more than the times have changed. *We* are different. The heady freedom my wife and I enjoy has an unhealthy side – the risk of a too conscious and constant attention to self. More choices mean more discussions of needs. With this kind of self-awareness, a selfish calculation can slip easily into even life's more intimate choices. In marriage, it tempts us to make deals rather than sacrifices.

The difference is a subtle but essential one.

When we seek deals in our intimate relationships – such as those of marriage and family – we allow the ethos of the market to spill over into our broader lives. In the idealized market, each leaves every transaction better off. But underlying the deal-making of the market is the isolated individual – one who begins his deal-making purged of the fragile, yet crucial ways we are connected to each other.

From such a perspective, the notion of sacrifice can only appear in a disparaging light – one my father would have difficulty recognizing. Obligations appear as external impositions rather than part of who we are. The sacrifices they involve thus become costs incurred rather than contributions to a meaningful life.

Now, my wife and I make deals all the time. Smaller deals in our daily routine – "you'll cook, I'll wash." Larger deals as we struggled with the basic arrangements of two careers and too much commuting. But these deals only work because of what undergirds them.

The magic of our marriage is the way it is giving us a different relationship to our own desires. They are no longer central to our satisfactions in the way they once were. Rather, in the rhythms of our intimacy, an essential alchemy occurs: giving becomes getting. As we each attend to the needs of the other, we are both, paradoxically, better off.

Thus, my wife and I are learning from each other something our parents couldn't teach us – how sacrifice works in our more open-textured world. Here amid our looser roles, it must be individually created and consciously chosen anew. Our parents couldn't teach us because they never understood this world enough, and we never understood them enough. They couldn't say it in a way we could hear it.

In the yelling matches of my teens and twenties, my father would tell me, "You always do exactly what you want." He meant it as a rebuke, but I saw it as a sign I was succeeding. Isn't that, I thought, what the good life is all about? Doing what you want to do? Whatever he was trying to say, I didn't get it then.

But marriage has changed me. I think I get it now.

Personal Reflection Prompts

1. In Chapter 2, on developing a holistic mind, we looked at the connection between happiness and having the right desires. In this essay, I acknowledge that marriage has changed me, fostering a new set of desires. Have any of your closest relationships, whether they be in marriage, family, or friends, altered your desires? Did any transform them for the better? Do you expect your more intimate relationships to change what you desire?
2. As the psychological dynamic of implicit egoism reveals, we tend to favor what is familiar to us. But through much of our lives, we are dealing with those whose experience is unfamiliar to us. Now that my wife and I are parents, we see how little of our parents' experience we could comprehend when we were children. Likewise, there is much that is unfamiliar to our parents about our lives amid "the looser roles of the new millennium." In your life, how do you work to empathize with the unfamiliar experiences of those you are closest to?
3. Have you ever been surprised with the way selfishness unwittingly slips into your life? Regarding yourself? Regarding others? Even in your most intimate relationships? Conversely, have there ever been times when you should have been more selfish in such relationships than you were?
4. Have you ever been in a relationship in which "giving becomes getting"? Can you offer some examples? Would you like to have more such relationships?
5. What role does sacrifice play in your life? When you do make a sacrifice, does it feel like a loss? Are there ways that the sacrifices you've made have enriched your life? How so? Would you make them again?
6. Beyond our more intimate relationships, we all have market relationships, buying and selling and producing. As employees. As consumers. As investors for our retirements. Do you find our market relationships leave everyone

"better off"? Have you ever mixed your intimate and market relationships? Lending money to a friend? Going into business with a relative? How did that work out? Would you do it again?

***

Developing the virtue of an empathetic heart can bring forth many positive, affirming relationships with other persons. But as the following essay acknowledges, it's the rare life that is only filled with such affirming positive relationships. For most of us, there are plenty of relationships that go the other way. But can an empathetic understanding help us deal with those annoying, yet unavoidable, persons in our lives? The following essay attempts an answer.

Complaining

If you'll indulge me, I need to complain about complainers.

I do so knowing there's always a danger of becoming what you criticize, and this concerns me. While I'm not above complaining, I don't want to become a complainer. There's a difference between saying critical things and becoming a critical person. The first I indulge in; the second I try to avoid.

Complainers wear on us because they're always taking from us. "Energy suckers," my friend calls them. We let them in only because they're such subtle robbers. They disguise their thievery as discourse.

They take from us in a variety of ways. If they're with us when we're relaxing, they take from us the pleasure of the moment. The restaurant could have been quieter, the movie funnier, and the parking easier.

When we encounter them at work, they take from us our accomplishments. They need the report changed, the shipment rerouted, and the meeting extended.

In romantic relationships, they're at their most destructive. We're too heavy, too emotional, too talkative, and too quiet.

The talk of complainers is, at bottom, a spiritual taking. It takes from us our transcendence. Complainers reduce us to our faults.

Granted, complaining has its attractions. For instance, it's a great attention-getter. You can sometimes even do it with a sense of pride, casting it as courage ("At least, I have the guts to speak up") or altruism ("I'm making the point for those that can't").

Complaining can also be a remedy for loneliness, providing entry into a group. This is where it's always been a particular temptation for me. Collective bitching and moaning is one of the primary ways we bind ourselves together. And the group offers a safe harbor for the complaining of the complainer. If everybody is doing it, nobody is one.

But even in these settings, there's something in a complainer that's less than legitimate. It's not simply that they're taking; it's the way they're taking. They're taking whether or not you're offering.

Complainers are always ill at ease, but particularly so when they're challenged. Thus, challenging them is rarely successful.

I once worked with a woman who regularly spent staff meetings criticizing whatever proposal was on the agenda. It didn't matter if the idea came from me, another coworker, or some outside party. She was, as someone said, an equal opportunity critiquer.

Frustrated by her behavior, I once began a meeting by asking my colleagues to start by first stating the positive aspects of the proposal we were discussing, leaving suggestions for changing it until the end. Visibly uncomfortable, she declined to comment, saying she wanted to hear what others had to say before speaking. After the others had spoken, she critiqued their comments. If she couldn't complain about the proposal, she would complain about others' comments about it!

Nowadays, I've learned my lesson. I don't try to counter complainers. I smile and let them go on. But I'm sure to keep all my spiritual valuables locked away.

The safe I've constructed consists of three rules. Two "don'ts" and a "do." I don't try to please them. I don't let them set the standards by which I evaluate other individuals or situations. I do try to see what I can learn from them.

It's the last rule that's the hardest to follow, particularly when the complainer's subject is someone you cherish or something you value. The first two rules provide you with protections from your weaknesses. The third requires you to draw upon your strength.

I'm helped with the third rule by remembering a general truth: a speaker is often telling you more about himself than his subject. The friend who thought the movie could have been funnier may have found it hit too close to home. The boss who wants the report changed may have a need to be in control. The spouse who complains about the quiet may have something to discuss.

The stronger I become, the more I can welcome the thieves in my life.

Sometimes, it's only when someone tries to steal something that you discover what's most worth saving.

Personal Reflection Prompts

1. In this chapter that focuses on developing and extending our empathy, it would be remiss not to acknowledge all the annoying people we have in our lives. I certainly have my share, and I suspect you do as well. How can the empathetic dispositions we are striving for here survive the daily array of irritations, nuisances, and "pain in the butts" we encounter? You have to be willing to play defense here. What are your defenses against your world's "energy suckers"?

2. Complaining has its personal pleasures, to be sure. When do you pleasurably indulge in complaining? What are the consequences when you do so? Have you ever regretted it? Complaining also has the potential to promote positive changes? In such cases, how do you effectively complain?
3. Is there a difference, as the essay asserts, "between saying critical things and becoming a critical person"?
4. Remember the philosopher Robert Solomon said that being part of a community involves becoming a "different person." As this essay points out, complaining can be a bonding experience, facilitating your entry into and acceptance by a community. But when "bitching and moaning" is the basis for a community, it usually is in opposition to something or someone else. Does the "different person" you become exclude empathy for the "opposition," however your community conceives it?
5. Do you feel you understand the interior lives of the complainers that frustrate you? What drives their behavior? Have you ever asked them? What was the result?
6. Can empathy be employed against complainers? If you can empathetically place yourself in the position of complainers, figure out what truly makes them tick, you might be able to manipulate them. Is empathy thus used strategically really empathy? In other words, does empathy have its less-than-noble uses?

4

Our Relationship with Things

An Attentive Eye

> "Absolute unmixed attention is a prayer."
>
> Simone Weil

Developing Your Attentive Eye

Unsimple Simplicity

The core aspiration of an attentive eye is simply a conscious and insightful awareness of the things in your world. But describing the virtue in this way risks being misunderstood. For developing this virtue is not simple in the sense of being effortless or easy. Indeed, as a fully realized practice, it is inherently challenging.

The virtue of an attentive eye is simple only in the sense of being unadulterated, as Simone Weil understood well. A reoccurring theme among my colleagues is the distracted nature of the students in their classrooms. My email box is full of articles and commentary by professors wrestling with the use of technology in their classrooms, particularly with the rapid development and transmission of machine learning and generative AI. But even before the growing prominence of large language models (LLMs) such as ChatGPT, department meetings were filled with conversations as to whether and to what degree to bring cell phones and YouTube into the classroom environment. Student claims regarding the efficacy of multi-tasking to the contrary, the research shows otherwise. Unmixed attention among us all is an increasingly rare commodity.

And if developing the virtue of an attentive eye includes not only a purity but also an expansion of your perception, there is an additional set of psychological complications. For, as we noted in Chapter 1's introduction, our attention is highly selective. We often miss things literally right before our eyes, even as psychological research shows, such obvious occurrences as a person in a gorilla suit or a clown on a unicycle wandering past. Learning should be not only lifelong but as a colleague recently told me, "lifewide," encompassing the totality of your world. An attentive eye is what enables this capacious outlook.

While I imperfectly embody all the virtues, the one I fail most frequently at is the virtue of an attentive eye. As this is the virtue I most regularly fall short of, I am fortunate to be married to a woman who excels in this regard. Whenever she says "Pay attention," I know to do a reset – I've avoided a number of mishaps with the guiderails she provides. More than one casserole has avoided being burnt in our oven because of her attentive eye.

While the development of this virtue requires significant efforts, the benefits of possessing this kind of awareness of the things in your world accumulate over time. Personally, I've seen this occur in a regular practice my family and I have adopted over the years. During dinner, we collectively pose to ourselves the question, "What do you know now that you didn't know when you woke up this morning?" This kind of practice of reflection can reinforce everyday learning as well as foster family intimacy. Though I should warn you, you could be surprised by what a spouse, sibling, or child might say. Perhaps something like: "Well, I learned today that Dad once again forgot to put down the toilet seat."

The benefits of an attentive eye have a particular relevance in your undertaking of moral exploration and growth. That's because the things in your world – the places you inhabit, the possessions you work for, and the practices you engage in – have a moral salience it is easy to overlook. While things, unlike persons, lack moral agency, they do have a moral tilt. They can encourage certain choices, attitudes, and stances and discourage others. Conscious attention to your practical engagements can help you from unwittingly becoming entangled with values you might not endorse upon further consideration.

Henry David Thoreau long ago recognized this, saying we've "become tools of our tools." As our tools become more sophisticated, Thoreau's insight has only become more profound. When he told his story of his life on Walden Pond, Thoreau didn't have to contend with the likes of email notifications or GPS directions or ChatGPT prompts. In one way or another, in telling your story today, you do.

Expanding Your Perceptions Outward

My friend Tim is a wise person. A Harvard-educated biologist, he is equally at home discussing plant ecology, William Wordworth's poetry, or the latest editorial in our local newspaper. Like many of us, he sends his relatives and friends a holiday letter with reflections on the just completed year.

This past year included a reflection on his enjoyment of bicycle riding. I'd like to quote at length an excerpt from his letter:

> "I started riding regularly during the warmer weather thirty years ago and have found it to be a delightful and beneficial way to keep an increasingly old and occasionally cranky body working reasonably well. I've also used a stationary bike indoors during the colder weather, either at a local fitness center or on a rear-wheel bike trainer at home. It works, but is far less stimulating than cruising the pavements under sunny skies, feeling the fresh air blow by, and actually getting somewhere for all the effort."

But this year, Tim's bike riding included an unexpected revelation:

> "Decades and thousands of miles later, on a balmy July morning this summer, on Pincherry Road north of the cabin, I suddenly realized a truth about my riding I had never noticed before that I dubbed 'the 30-foot syndrome.' Most of the time – 70% or more, it seems – I focus my visual field on the oncoming thirty-or-so feet of road in my lane to be sure I'm not surprised by an unexpected frost crack, pothole, manhole cover, loose gravel, broken glass, downed branch, dead animal, manure pile (in Lancaster County, for sure) or sundry object that has fallen off of, or has been tossed out of a vehicle."

He then continues:

> "There is a different kind of risk in the 30-foot syndrome, however, and this is what surprised me in July when I looked up, scanning the farther 180-degree view ahead and left to right, and it dawned on me that I was not really seeing the full landscape as I zipped along. And I had done this for years!"

And then Tim poses the question that gave me pause as I read his letter:

> "I had ridden the same routes many, many times, and naturally had become familiar with their general features. I had 'seen it all already,' so what was the problem? Knowing the route well increases the safety margin. Was I missing, something, and if so, how important was it?"

When Tim moves from his 30-feet-ahead to the 180-degree view he is expanding his perception in the way that developing an attentive eye is designed to foster. And he rightly asks a question it would behoove all of us to ask in our lives: What had he been missing and how important was it?

Amid the practical pressures of everyday life, we regularly assume a focused, yet blinkered view. And many times, it is a wise and necessary choice. You don't want to hit a pothole while riding a bike. You also don't want to forget your umbrella on a rainy day, overlook your child's running nose, miss your spouse's birthday, or fail to proofread that client update going out tomorrow. But there are dangers – and often of the more profound sort – if you don't on occasion ask: What am I missing? If I adopted a different angle of vision, what would I see?

A Doing-something-different Challenge

In this regard, I've taken on a practice that I now regularly employ. The task is a straightforward one, at least initially. Looking over your daily routines, I'd like you to take a different route than your accustomed one to wherever you're going. The change can be as small or large as you like. I remember once taking on this challenge myself, deciding to walk a different way across campus from the parking lot to my office. That's when I came across the hidden art studios my college had, filled with half-finished creative projects that would regularly take my breath away. Even on a campus I had crossed for years, I found there was plenty I was missing. I'm betting that even amid your familiar routines, you'll find that too.

Expanding Your Perceptions Inward

Expanding your perceptions can occur into different directions. My friend Tim's bicycle story is about expanding your angle of vision, taking in a wider view that was previously constrained. Thus, by its very nature, this is an expansion of perception outward. As Tim's story reveals, a previously constrained vision can often happen unconsciously, never rising to the level of awareness. With an awareness of the constraint, you can, as Tim did, make an intentional choice to do otherwise, expanding your perception outward and widening the scope of the world you hope to engage.

You can also expand your perceptions inward. With this kind of expansion, your aim is not to adopt a broader angle of vision. Expanding your perceptions inward instead involves seeing anew what is already in your line of sight. It is to engage more closely and carefully – more intimately – with your present scope of observation.

You learn different things with telescopes than microscopes, yet each offers insights into your world, displaying things that were previously obscured. Both can make the world more interesting and neither can be ignored. By way of analogy, the same can be said of outward and inward expansion of your perception. They both open up new horizons you wouldn't want to miss.

Using Your Imagination

It may seem paradoxical, but using your imagination can be a great way to expand your perceptions inward. It can seem so because while expanding your perceptions inward involves greater attention to your experience of your immediate surroundings, your imagination aims to take you to a different mental location. Your imagination enables your immersion in a creatively constructed world of your own choosing.

But much depends on how you use your imagination's creativity. The key thing to understand is this: Your imagination's power to imagine *not* seeing something can sharpen and deepen your appreciation of seeing something. For example, if I imagine for a moment losing three of my fingers – it's unsettling even to think of this – I immediately gain a renewed appreciation when I look and see with a bit of relief my complete and well-functioning hand. Revealingly, as I write this sentence, I find myself unexpectedly wiggling my fingers with a new-found pleasure. We too often appreciate things only after they are gone.

But using your imagination well, you can appreciate them while they're here. And that applies not simply to seeing, but to your other senses as well: hearing, tasting, smelling, and touching.

Recall the monk that when asked what he had done over the years, pointed outside his window and simply said, "I watched that flower grow." He was sensitively attuned to subtle changes in the plant's appearance – the bursting forth of a new bud, for instance – because through his well-developed and finely-honed imagination, he could recall the plant as it was before this bud emerged. And going back even further in years: He could bring to mind the emptiness of a vacant spot outside his window before the blossoming flower came into existence. It is in imagining the world without the flower that its current incarnation comes most vividly into view.

Try this yourself. Reflect upon any particularly memorable experience from your past as fully and deeply as you can. Let your reflection range freely. Your infant daughter's first step. That cold beer on a hot day. The sweet smell of a fresh-cut grass. Hearing a gentle rain on your roof as you go off to sleep. The softness of that first kiss.

Then, imagine your world suddenly stripped of that memorable experience. What if you missed your daughter's first step because you were on your phone? Imagining the regret of such a moment might prompt you today to watch her more closely at the playground, wondering what surprise could come next. What if years ago fearing rejection, you never risked that first kiss of the person who became your lifelong partner? Imagining the unsettling absence of your partner might incline you this morning to give him or her an extra hug. By now imaginatively experiencing what you would have missed, you are better equipped to encounter that person anew.

You need to learn how to see things *as if* you are seeing them for the first time.

You are up against the hedonic treadmill we mentioned earlier. Experiences we encounter regularly tend to fade into the background. They become an assumed baseline that needs to be exceeded in order to have the same effects the original experience once provided.

The danger of the habitual is the way it can deaden your experience. Like any drug taken every day, it will lose its potency.

***

We can often try to solve this problem by injecting novelty into our lives. The profitability of many businesses depends on this. That's often the allure of travel, for instance. Look at any travel website and it is full of promises for experiencing new people, locales, cultures, and foods. Certainly, for most of us, going on an African safari or climbing Mount Everest would shake things up.

I regularly look forward to my next trip. Travel is one of life's elevating experiences. One of my favorite quotes in this regard comes from Mark Twain: He wrote, "Travel is fatal to prejudice, bigotry, and narrow-mindedness, and many of our people need it sorely on these accounts. Broad, wholesome, charitable views of men and things cannot be acquired by vegetating in one little corner of the earth all one's lifetime."

What Twain does not say here (though his sharp observations elsewhere make clear he would appreciate it) is how much elevation is possible if one attends more carefully to one's "little corner of the earth." This can happen whenever you look at your accustomed surroundings with new eyes. You can travel even when you are sitting in your favorite easy chair.

It pays on occasion to adopt the stance of the monk and look carefully around. What have you often looked at, but never seen? More than African safaris, that is the bounty of your life.

Possessions, Practices, Places

Nudges

Psychologists have long known that the things in our lives – the possessions, practices, and places – provide "behavioral cues" or nudges that prompt us to behave in one way or another. Scholars Richard H. Thaler and Cass R. Sunstein in their book *Nudges*, for instance, relate how simply repositioning the food in a school cafeteria can encourage healthier eating habits among students.

Thus, it is not surprising to have Wall Street Journal columnist, Michelle Slatalla, pen a column "If I'm Sober-Curious, Do I Have to Toss My Bar Cart?" noting that walking by the cart in the early evening tempts her to fix a drink, even when she wants to cut back on her alcohol consumption. Because things as ordinary as a bar cart can encourage our choices in a variety of ways, they regularly embody moral tilts. Yet precisely because of their commonplace nature, such moral tilts often escape our attention.

Possession and a Culture of More

Your possessions, your stuff, even the clutter around you, help to give your life its personal character and distinctive shape. Thus, just as your relationships with other persons are deserving of your ethical reflection, so your relationship with things merits your thoughtful inquiry.

This is more so because of the variety of stuff that readily becomes part of our lives in a materialistic and consumer-oriented culture. In significant measure, "Lifestyles of the Rich and Famous" is a hit show because it gives us access to the possession-filled lives of the well-to-do. I'll confess too that even I (whom my wife sometimes half-jokingly describes as someone who could happily live in a box) regularly scan the weekend mansion section of the Wall Street Journal, gawking at the multimillion-dollar homes I will never be able to afford.

This wide exposure to the varied possessions of others readily inculcates in us a pervasive mind-set of comparison. We are more inclined nowadays to compare ourselves not simply to our family members or neighbors, but to the uber-wealthy such as Elon Musk, Bill Gates, and Warren Buffett. But this compulsion to compare can lead to some surprising results. Research on happiness shows, for example, folks living in a $300,000 house in a neighborhood with $200,000 houses are happier than those living in a $400,000 house in an environment of $500,000 houses. From a detached, outside perspective, this culture of more can be riddled with such paradoxes.

Quantitative Measurements and Qualitative Judgments

But there is more than the culture of more to our possessions. Not all possessions are created equal and their value can't always be captured by a common denominator, such as their market value. Legally, for instance, the family dog I grew up with, Bonnie, was property. But her value to my family far exceeded the dollar cost at the time of a miniature collie.

Consistent with our materialistic culture, our legal system struggles with how to compensate for the loss of noneconomic value. I regularly pose to my students the question of how much financial compensation should a dog owner receive if his dog is killed by a negligent driver. This is something my students struggle with a great deal. They want to say more than the dog's market value, but they are at a loss as to how to measure this "more." They struggle for words, uncertain as to the appropriate language. The best they can do is tell personal stories – often moving ones when they speak with deep emotion of their pets. Yet in a lawsuit context, they worry that their reactions are idiosyncratic and overly subjective when confronted by an impersonal legal analysis.

Asking the Why Question
Coming to terms with your relationship to things as part of an undertaking of moral exploration begins by asking the "Why" question. Why do you value a particular possession of yours? Embedded in the "Why" question is often the more specific query of what kind of value do you assign to your possession?

When I think about the "Why" behind purchasing a new car, I see many reasons surfacing among people I know. Reflecting upon the "Why's" here reveals a variety of moral tilts in play. I know one mechanically-inclined person who would love to buy a new car every year. His "Why" is rooted is a curiosity and deep fascination with the increasing complexities and capacities of engineering advances. Thus, the moral tilt of a new car for him is the way it fosters new dimensions of curiosity and the desire for technical learning. Then, there is the person purchasing a high-end flashy car in the $100,000 range who enjoys giving his friends rides and driving conspicuously around town. The moral tilt of this high-end car tends toward a need to impress others in his crowd. A third person buys a car because of its reputed longevity and safety record. For her, it reinforces a moral tilt toward keeping her family and children safe.

It is even the case that the moral tilt of car purchases can run in diametrically opposed ways among different groups. When I practiced law, attorneys of my acquaintance often favored newer, expensive cars, subtly telegraphing their success to potential clients. Yet a group of engineers I knew took a contrasting pride in keeping older, run-down cars going beyond the car's typical years of operation, thus exhibiting their technical skill and know-how.

Personalizing the "Why" Question
As part of your undertaking of moral exploration, take some time to do a survey of your possessions. Strive to incorporate some variety into your choices. Thus, you may love the many oil paintings you have carefully and tastefully arranged throughout your home, but don't include only paintings in your survey.

If asked to reflect upon their possessions, individuals often call to mind typical household items such as cars, cloths, furniture, and televisions. My students are deeply attached to their phones. When I playfully asked how much they'd have to be paid to give up their phones for a week, their responses were often in the hundreds of dollars. Professors like myself often have a fondness for books. (So much so that in my case, my wife has taken to discouraging me from acquiring any more. I've learned that my "We all have our addictions" protestation is a losing argument).

But in considering your possessions, try to move beyond the belongings that most typically come to mind. What are the possessions that more distinctly bear your personal imprint? Is it that set of tools your father left you in his will? Is it the homemade card your five-year-old gave you for your birthday? Is it that old easy chair that fits you just right? Is it that tree outside your window that you planted years ago as a sapling?

Then, consider your relationship to the belonging you have chosen. Of the possession you are reflecting upon, ask the "Why" question. Why do you value this particular thing? What associations or memories does it bring to mind? What thoughts or feelings surface as you linger over it? How would you describe its meaning for you to someone else? In contemplating questions such as these, the moral tilts of items reveal themselves.

Let me give you an example from my own life. One of my possessions that is deeply meaningful for me is a silver pocket watch my father gave to me a number of years back. It was the watch his father gave to him. My dad's father died when my dad was around 12 years old, so he didn't know him for much of his life. I never knew my grandfather, but my dad always had this silver watch.

It now sits under glass in one of our bedrooms. As far as I know, it no longer runs. But as I look it over from time to time, that doesn't matter.

I remember clearly the moment my dad gave this watch to me, one of the few things he had from his father. Its moral tilt for me lay in my father's loving gesture to me of a gift of one of his most prized possessions. The moral tilt was one of love – my father's love of me and my reciprocal love of him. The attitude it evokes for me is one of the permanent and abiding possibilities of love, across generations, across time. It stays with me, even though my dad passed away several years ago. It continues to affect my choices and daily comportment with a bias toward love, even when it's hard, even when my immediate reactions are far from loving.

It also fosters in me a sense of respect for those who came before me, of what they overcame, as immigrants who arrived with little in the way of money or education. It entails a sense of connection going back farther than I can know in any detail. The moral tilt for me here is one of appreciation and gratitude. It's helped to foster in me a desire to pay things forward. Quite a lot, I know, for a watch that can't even still tell time.

You Have More Possessions Than You Know
In reflecting upon the moral tilts of your possessions – what they foster and what they impede – you need not limit yourself to possessions of a material nature. Indeed, the moral tilts of your nonmaterial possessions can often be more impactful. You can possess hope. You can possess regrets. You can possess confidence. You can possess fears. Each of these can push you in one direction or another.

They can influence your choices, inform your values. Over time, they can become an intimate part of your makeup, your character.

These immaterial possessions are things too and figuring out the moral tilts in your relationship to them is part of who you are. So, what are your immaterial possessions? Especially the ones that others can't see. And which ways are they morally tilting?

Practices

The practices in our lives run deep. They can have a casual, everyday air, such as a quiet, solitary routine of enjoying your morning cup of coffee to the emotionally arresting recitation of your marriage vows before friends and family. In my own life, interestingly enough, these two practices had an unexpected affinity. Prior to marrying my wife, I was a committed tea drinker. But after many mornings of encountering the seductive aromas of my wife brewing her morning coffee, I succumbed to the temptation, and I will say, happily so. Both my morning coffee and my supportive wife continue to bring new dimensions to my life.

Each of these initial practices has a moral tilt, fostering tendencies that may have always been there, even if not consciously considered. The moral tilt of my morning coffee is one of a self-centering moment, as I process my thoughts and prepare for the day. I am, as they say, "getting myself together," and the tilt is toward a deeper peace, steadfastness, resilience, and a predilection toward positively taking on whatever the day might bring. As my family is well aware, you will almost always get a better response from after-coffee me than from before-coffee me.

While my practice of a morning coffee is largely a solitary affair, reciting my marriage vows was a much more social practice, and its moral tilts followed accordingly. Most fundamentally, of course, the moral tilt was toward my wife. This declaration of my marriage vows –at once intimate and public – embodied a moral tilt of commitment to her and an array of implicit promises of fidelity and care. Most prominently for me was the putting of the welfare of another person before my own.

There was also a larger communal moral tilt that day because of the presence of my parents. By making them an integral part of the ceremony, I was showing them the adult I hoped to be, one worthy not only of their love but also of their respect and admiration. This is something I am still trying to live up to.

Taking in the Array of Practices

In engaging practices as part of an undertaking of moral reflection and development, it's first important to become more fully aware of the practices that are part of your life. There are likely practices that you never thought of as such. Yet their moral significance nonetheless informs your life in subtle and significant ways.

Private Routines

Some of your practices are never visible to anyone else. I would, before teaching a class, for instance, always repeat a silent mantra to myself: "Be clear, be engaging, be honest, be kind." At the moment I'm writing this, I realize I don't believe I've ever previously told this habitual mantra to anyone else, even though through the years I saw it as an important personal practice for the teacher I aspired to be. It is full of moral tilts that I wished to bring to my relationships with my students. Clarity. Engagement. Honesty. Kindness.

Do you have any such private mental practices? It could be the mental checklist you go through before a family trip to make sure you haven't forgotten anything that anyone may need. The moral tilt here is an expression of concern for the well-being of your family members.

As an athlete, it could be that choice of a particular song to stream via your earbuds before the game. The same song before every contest. Sure, it's a bit of a superstition that you only half-believe. But you do it every time as you've learned it mentally prepares you for the competition. The moral tilt here is one that strengthens your desire to do your personal best.

It could be that pause you've started doing before you leave an elderly parent or friend, all too aware that it may be the last time you will see them. You take a moment and look them over carefully, surveying their features. Noting the look on their face, their posture in the chair, how their chest rises and lowers as they breathe, and gradually drift off to sleep. The moral tilt here is toward the importance of remembrance, of honoring all that's come before.

It could be that silent prayer you utter before any business speech or presentation, asking of whatever you regard as a higher power, "Don't let me screw up." The moral tilt here is a belief in something beyond yourself and an acknowledgement of your need for spiritual support.

Group Rituals

I remember being introduced to a Polish tradition on Christmas Eve as I was welcomed into my wife's family after our marriage. Before a special meal (a delicious one –I can almost taste it as I write these words), the family would gather, each member taking a wafer. We would then circulate offering a piece of our own wafer to each of the other members of the family. The ritual reaffirmed our connection, expressing a hope to ensure health and happiness in the coming year.

What are your group rituals and what moral tilts do they embody?

It could be the "mandatory fun" of office exercises and outings. They are never meant to be merely enjoyable. They might be aimed at increasing trust and communication among coworkers. They could hope to inspire commitment to a new corporate venture. They might be designed to relieve the pressure of a stressful work environment.

It might be your annual family vacation, going off to a particular locale every summer. A trip the kids used to love, but now they want to bring along their teenage friends or perhaps even skip it altogether for a getaway with their college roommates. Thus, you need to be aware of how the moral tilts of the same group practice can change over time.

Social Practices

I remember when my daughter accompanied me to the polling place to vote in her first presidential election. Truth be told, I've always enjoyed voting. There is something about doing this practice together. I like bumping into my neighbors there. I like that I can share a friendly chat about our kids with a guy a block over, even though I suspect he will vote differently from me. The moral tilt here is a commitment to the common good, even though we may define it in markedly different ways. It reinforces a realization that in a deeper way we are all in this together, even if only in our aspirations. Having my daughter with me enriched the many dimensions of this moral tilt. I realized her new adult status and her shared equality with me as an age-of-majority voter. Her opinions will never again be those of a child.

Robert Putnam's *Bowling Alone* is now old news, but the growing disconnection we have from each other is not. His book detailed our declining civil engagement and our lessening participation in everything from PTAs to churches to political parties. Today, we appear more distrustful and polarized than ever. Bonding with like-minded groups, but suspicious of those beyond them. The bridges that formerly spanned our differences appear more tenuous and uncertain.

In such a world, we should attend more carefully to our practices, whether they are of a private, group, or social character. We need to look more closely at how they can bring us together and how they can force us apart – and ask how we can do them better.

Places

My father had a saying he would regularly voice during his working days: It had variations, but it always went something like this: "Somehow, when you get to Maine, everything is alright." As we grew older, Maine was where we would go for holidays and family vacations. For my dad, Maine was the place where he broke free of the corporate grind. He loved, as do I, the state's independent streak. It's a place that doesn't stand on formality or pretense. It allows you to do your own thing, accepting of the idiosyncrasies we all have and willing to "live and let live." After my dad's retirement, he and my mother moved there on a permanent basis.

Why do places have these holds on us? For my dad, Maine was better than any therapy he could have paid for. The places that have this impact are varied with often different effects upon each of us. As a southern counterpart to Maine, my grandfather used to say his move to Florida added ten years to his life.

The connection between place and behavior has been the subject of much psychological study. Writer Malcom Gladwell, in his book *Talking to Strangers*, describes the phenomenon of "coupling." "Coupling," he writes, "is the idea that behaviors are linked to very specific circumstances and conditions." In his own life, Gladwell recalls how his father while "not someone whose emotions bubbled over," nonetheless wept in the household setting of reading Charles Dickens's *A Tale of Two Cities* to Gladwell and his brother when they were kids.

So, why this coupling effect? On the surface at least, my dad looked the same as he always did, yet particularly after Maine became his permanent residence, he was different. More relaxed. More emotional. More open to exploration. This is because my dad, like all of us, was far from the detached and autonomous actor some economic theories espouse us to be. We are all embedded in the environments we inhabit. They exercise subtle and not-so-subtle influences on our attitudes, decisions, and development.

But while knowing this intuitively, we seldom subject these places to the sustained ethical reflection the merit, such as Gladwell does with crime in exploring how we interact with strangers. It's often easy to see this influence upon others, in the way parents, for instance, readily take note of the negative influences over their children. It is much harder to discern this influence for ourselves in whatever environment we presently inhabit. As the old saying goes, "Fish don't recognize the water." And we all have our "fish' moments.

As I did before with possessions and practices, I'll give you an example of a place from my own life, one I've often valued, but continue to deepen my understanding of and suspect I haven't touched bottom yet.

My parent's place in Maine was on a lake and they had built a dock extending out into the water. While the dock was anchored, it would rock gently with the ripples of the lake water underneath it. Looking out over the water, the dock faced east and thus in the early morning was suffused by the most beautiful sunrises. As the sun rose, it's reflection in the water would glimmer, breaking into little diamond-like reflections across the lake. Many mornings, I would sit on the dock, sipping my coffee and taking in the unfolding scene.

Or perhaps better put, letting the scene take me in. For immersed in this scene, my mind would regularly go places I didn't expect or couldn't immediately understand.

At first, a peaceful sensation would wash over me. I could feel my muscles relax and my breathing slow. Kind of like sinking into a hot bath, even though there was no external change in temperature. It was less a physical and more an emotional balm. Thus, in its own way, it was more deeply soothing.

This is the place where I've done some of my own best reflecting. In my dock experiences, I pondered everything from health issues to lost friendships, from career choices to home moves, from future hopes to missed opportunities. And always, I came away with some particular insight or resolution for moving forward. Indeed, even now, years later, I can imaginatively recall the scene and the thoughts flow once again.

Your Places of Insight

So, where are your places of insight? You might think of them simply as the places you go when your wobbly moments begin to overwhelm you.

Where do all the clamors and pressures of your day fade, if only momentarily? Where is your sanctuary for making sense of the jumble of thoughts and feelings that take up much of your time? Where is your still spot in your moving world?

It could be wherever you turn off your phone. It could be that hot bath. It could be the moment before everyone else gets up. It could be that walk up a deserted trail. It could be staring at the moon. It could be in a house of worship. It could be in bed under the covers. It could be holding your child. Wherever the specifics of the locale, it's the place where peace and insight come.

Wherever your places of insight may be, I hope you come to value them. The time you give them is a better investment than compulsively checking the financial news or tracking Robinhood's latest meme stock. For the value embedded in such places is not a bigger bank account, but a better you.

Artificial Intelligence

Of all the things in our world, the rapid advance and pervasiveness of new technologies stand out in sharp relief. This is, in part, because these technologies – from Tiktok to the Metaverse to ChatGPT – are things across the three senses of things we have been considering. They are certainly possessions – think of the cell phones that now rarely leave our sides. But the possession of a cell phone also immerses us in practices – regularly, even compulsively, scrolling through TikTok, for instance. And collectively, these new technologies are a place, in fact, a distinctive place that displaces us. Indeed, that is part of the singular appeal of the Metaverse, the ability to leave your immediate physical surroundings behind and navigate a plethora of imaginative worlds of great variety.

Like all technologies, these newer ones have a variety of moral tilts. They can, often subtly, push us in one way or another, affecting our choices and ultimately over time the persons we become. That was recognized long before the advent of the internet. Remember Thoreau's caution. We've "become tools of our tools." They are thus worthy of serious ethical reflection.

In using these technologies, what values are you accepting? What conceptions of the good life are you, implicitly at least, adopting and endorsing? And when you look closely, do you like what you see?

Early on, even some of those associated with the development of these newer technologies were issuing warnings. In *You Are Not a Gadget*, Jaron Lanier wrote, "I fear that we are beginning to design ourselves to suit digital models of us," adding we "have repeatedly demonstrated our species' bottomless ability to lower our standards to make information technology look good." How are we designing ourselves to suit the digital expectations in our lives? Are we lowering our standards to make information technology look good? I am now regularly tempted to use Google's prominently displayed AI summaries, rather than researching a topic or question more thoroughly.

The more recent advent and rapid advances in generative AI and machine learning only make such inquiries more pressing. And there is certainly much more to come. In his book *Co-Intelligence: Living and Working with AI,* Ethan Mollick argues we should assume our current tools are the worst artificial intelligence (AI) we will ever use. Mollick says he expects AI to continue to develop, potentially exponentially.

While we certainly need to attend to the rapidly deployed array of new tech options, we should realize even the hype of the moment could be misleading. It is worth today recalling Amara's law, coined by scientist and futurist Roy Amara. As he put it, "We tend to overestimate the effect of a technology in the short run and underestimate the effect in the long run." So, we need to look beyond the superficial froth to the more substantial potential for change.

With this goal in mind, your undertaking of moral reflection is the ideal lens. For our ethics are at the core of who we are, comprising our fundamental values and aspirations. It's where we can attend to technology's deeper impact.

Certainly, there is no lack of informed (not to mention uninformed) commentary on the deeper ways that technology is transforming our core selves. For instance, Jonathan Haidt, in his book *The Anxious Generation*, sees smart phones as behind the worrisome increase of mental health struggles among children and adolescents.

As we're seen throughout our undertaking, choices develop into habits that evolve into character. Thus, in developing any virtue, it is wise to start with what is readily at hand.

So, agree or disagree with Haidt, one place to begin to develop your attentive eye, is with a reflective look at the phone that, at this moment, if you're like most of us, is in all probability within reach. What do you see?

The Moral Risks of Your Moral Tilts

Discerning Moral Risks

Thus far, we have been largely looking at moral tilts in terms of their potential for positive moral impact. As we have seen, such impacts of possessions, practices, and places are varied and wide-ranging. A wedding ring on your finger can be a reminder and daily reinforcement of fidelity and commitment. A practice of writing "Thank you" notes tilts toward developing a comportment of appreciation and gratitude. A stable and quiet place to read can prompt the development of imagination and curiosity in a youngster for years to come.

As part of an undertaking of moral exploration and growth, such an initial emphasis on the potential of the things in your world for moral elevation is entirely appropriate. But the same things that can be morally uplifting can also bring with them an array of moral risks.

In an undertaking of this nature, it's often important to look at the ways in which initially good things can turn bad, how even honorable commitments may take unexpected turns. This is where the more morally subtle risks arise. Its where we can go wrong without ever being aware we've done so. As a working ethicist, I've encountered my share of executives who were part of some of the biggest ethical scandals, from Enron to Theranos to FTX, yet who at the time they made their decisions honestly believed they were doing nothing unethical. Indeed, they didn't even perceive their decisions as being ethical in nature, but rather economic, managerial, or organizational choices.

Misfocused: The Distortion of Attention

It is often some of the best parts of ourselves that give rise to committed pursuits.

The startup entrepreneur working late, sleeping in his office, hoping for the big payoff that would offer financial security for his family. The ambitious high school student taking multiple AP courses along with demanding extracurricular activities in hopes of getting into a top college. Both of them are undoubtedly engaged in worthy pursuits with commendable goals. But absorbed by his start-up's demands, the entrepreneur learns too late he failed to appreciate his son's growing drug dependencies. Tired, overburdened, and anxious, the high school student succumbs one night to the temptation to cheat on a take-home exam.

This dynamic can happen with individuals who have the highest ideals. Indeed, such individuals may have a particular vulnerability in this regard. I recall a deeply religious minister who worked tirelessly for his congregation realizing later in life that he had "only left the crumbs" for his relationship with his wife.

Ideals can inspire us, but they can also unbalance us.

Philosopher Kenneth E. Goodpaster coined a term for the singular pursuit of one goal to the exclusion of others. He called it "teleopathy." In his words: "Teleopathy is the unbalanced pursuit of purpose by either individuals or organizations." He saw it as a particular risk for those in a business environment, describing it as "an occupational hazard of business life and the key stimulus to which business ethics is a response."

But the unbalanced pursuit of singular goals is hardly restricted to business. It is a dynamic to which we are all subject. It can often be easy to recognize in others from afar. But because of the way it is intertwined with our own praiseworthy pursuits, it can be harder to recognize in ourselves. That deeply committed minister always had a ready rationalization for missing evening meals with his wife.

Teleopathy in Your Own Life?

As part of your ethical reflection, try this exercise in your own life. What are the things in your life you jealously protect? The kind of things that you would get nervous or testy about should anyone question their value or appropriateness. Consider places you inhabit. It could be that weekly poker game you never miss. Consider the possessions you work for. Perhaps that new luxury car in your driveway. Consider the practices you engage in. That early morning workout you refuse to miss.

Like the above examples, the things that come to your mind might well be in themselves innocuous or even beneficial. The sociability of friends playing cards. A new car that saves you from repair bills. The physical exercise that helps keep you healthy.

But recalling the innocuous or beneficial aspects of these things is only part of the process of ethical reflection here – and let's be honest, it's the easy part. The next step involves asking: What do you give up or pass over or otherwise marginalize in your life on account of those things? Did the weekly poker game mean you missed a phone call from your elderly parent? Does the luxury car purchase mean you might be failing to save enough for your retirement? Did that morning workout mean you rushed off without helping your neighbor when his dog broke loose?

Given the finite creatures that we are, we are limited in time, attention, and energy. Thus, attending to one thing inevitably involves not attending to something else. No matter how much we wish to believe otherwise, no one really does it all. This truth is worthy of more moral reflection than many of us typically give it. Particularly with those things in which we've heavily invested, we also are not often well positioned to do this reflection entirely on our own.

This is one of the reasons we need each other. So, in this ethical reflection, include a check-in with those whose judgment you trust, including those who love you enough to tell you even what you may not want to hear.

Unfocused: The Distraction of Attention

Simone Weil's quote at the head of this chapter spoke of "absolute unmixed attention." As any college professor will tell you nowadays, that kind of attention is increasingly hard to come by.

Reflecting upon how students have changed in her twenty years of teaching, Rebecca Vidra, a senior lecturer at Duke University, recently wrote:

> "When I lecture, I look out to a sea of stickered laptops, with students shifting their attention between me, my slides and their screens. I remind them that I can tell when they are watching TikTok or texting, because the class material probably isn't causing their amused facial expressions."

Along with her distracted students, she also finds herself being distracted. "Honestly, I am finding myself more distracted, too. While lecturing, I am not only thinking about the lecture material and what's on the next slide – I am also wondering how I can get my students' attention."

Discerning Purpose

While instructors today more frequently encounter the disruption and dispersal of student attention, I've also, in my teaching, encountered a countertrend: Students today are also receptive, even eager, to finding larger purposes that engage and animate them. Instructors should tap into and develop this desire more than we typically do. As William Sullivan in *Liberal Learning as a Quest for Purpose* notes: "The trajectory of today's students' personal lives and careers has become increasingly uncertain. This has caused rising levels of anxiety. For these students, elevating the exploration of a life worth living into a major focus of their undergraduate education is a great benefit."

Other higher education scholars too have emphasized the remarkable role engaging students in the question of their purpose can play in their education. Tim Clydesdale in *The Purposeful Graduate*, for instance, details how engaging students about their vocational calling has numerous educational benefits, from enriching their intellectual development to increasing their community involvement to promoting a focus on their larger life aims.

Such educational findings provide a clue as to how we might more intentionally live our adult lives, even when our years of formal schooling are behind us. In a world marked by an increasing disruption of our attention, redoubling our commitment to reflecting upon our life's purpose has a deeper salience. It may provide precisely the kind of psychological guardrail you need, especially during your pressured or hectic days. Far from being a youthful exercise, the discernment of purpose is an ongoing task that you can sharpen and extend throughout your life.

As the Stoic philosopher Seneca wrote, "When a man does not know what harbor he is making for, no wind is the right wind." In other words, without discerning your purpose, you'll lack a dependable basis for the choices you are making. That is an open invitation to distractions and the enervating dispersal of your attention.

Of course, you could take the perspective of the Cheshire Cat in Lewis Carroll's *Alice in Wonderland*: If you don't know where you are going any road will take you there.

But I'd bet on Seneca.

Recognizing Your Distractions

So, the more fundamental task in dealing with the many tempting distractions that the things in your life provide is discerning your purpose. For discerning your purpose shapes your understanding of the nature and scope of your life's distractions. It helps you to recognize them. This is because a distraction is a distraction only in relation to something else, something of greater importance, meaning, or value. In this way, discerning your purpose is a way of regaining your focus.

Discovering your purpose is the work of an open spirit, the virtue we shall turn to in the next chapter. It is the paramount step in forming an answer to the question posed at the beginning of this moral venture, asking of yourself, "What is the story that I wish to tell about myself?"

Topical Reflections

But first, just as we did with our relationships with ourselves and others, let's consider some topical reflections delving into our relationships with things.

***

In this first essay, I deal with all the things in my life that I euphemistically refer to as "details." They are the not-terribly-inspiring, yet inevitably have-to-be-done practices in my life. These are the run-of-the-mill hassles that we seldomly think of as practices, but this stuff can affect significantly the quality of our days.

Details

I have a way of summing up the stuff of life – the laundries, the lawn mowings, the mortgage payments; the trips to the dentist, the post office, the car mechanic; stops for gas, for money, for cough medicine. My shorthand for all this like-it-or-not-it-still-needs-to-be-done stuff is "details." And as the old saying goes, the devil is certainly in them.

I've spent my life running from details – cutting them back, handing them off, doing them too quickly, or rationalizing away their need to be done.

And lately I've noticed: Many of my peers are doing the same thing. An increasingly popular DoorDash service, for example, replacing shopping for and cooking a family dinner. We wanted to have it all. Now, we're figuring out how to handle it.

Simplicity in its own way is complex. This is because you don't want simply to simplify; you want to simplify well. And this entails more than cutting back on details. It entails coming to understand why you've been running from them in the first place.

The details of our lives don't simply exist "out there," appearing suddenly like potholes in the road as we round a curve. Rather, we construct the details in our lives slowly over time, often unwittingly.

The essence of a detail lies in its own derivative status. It's something instrumentally rather than intrinsically good. We get satisfaction from a detail only by having gotten it done. Thus, the satisfaction of doing my laundry is slipping into clean clothes; the pleasure of a stop at an ATM is money in my pocket.

But given their instrumental character, details necessarily point to the more central values in our lives. Cough medicine fosters the health I cherish. Details emerge in the particular sense of like-it-or-not-they-still-need-to-be-done stuff only after we've come to regard something other in our lives as worthy in itself.

And here's the secret: If we can construct details, we can also reconstruct them.

We all have our priority ladders, the hierarchy of values by which we organize our lives. Recognized or not, they underlie our perceptions of what is important and what is not.

I recall a partner in my law firm running frantically down the hall one evening, asking if anyone knew how to run the copy machine. His administrative assistant was gone for the day and the negotiation of a complex business deal had suddenly come to a halt because he was unable to provide the other side with a hard copy of a requested document. At that moment, his ladder wobbled. Something he never thought of as important had become so.

To reconstruct the details of our lives, we need to wobble our ladders. We need to ask whether what we have come to regard as important in our lives is in fact so.

When I do this, I often discover another unwitting hierarchy. And when I inspect the damage it's done, the injury is startlingly clear. In each case, I've divided up my life and relegated a part of it to insignificance.

Achieving simplicity in my life is more fundamentally about renewing engagements than reducing them. The essential first step is learning how to honor *all* my activities.

Doing so is for me an act of recovery, an exercise in seeing something I missed the first time around. I find myself going back further than I expected, back before I was a professional, back even before college. Discovering something I see now only in retrospect from a memory during my teenage years. Back then, I could have learned something about finding pleasure in whatever I was doing from someone even younger than myself.

As a teenager I had to watch over a young boy I'll call Donnie, when a group of us all went together to the beach. Looking forward to all the other activities the waterfront offered, I was restless. To keep Donnie occupied, I would draw a line in the sand and tell him to follow it to the end. The line I drew turned and twisted, doubled back and went forward, covering a long stretch of beach. It then ultimately came full circle, returning to the place where it began. Donnie would follow the line all over the beach, enjoying its wanderings, circling around, and each time discovering its contours anew. He would do this for nearly an hour at a time.

Back then, I chuckled at what Donnie didn't see, how all his efforts got him nowhere. Now, looking back, I'm dismayed at what I was missing. Sitting still, I was restless and already running. Galloping around the beach, Donnie was exactly where he wanted to be.

Personal Reflection Prompts

1. This essay brings into view how "The Culture of More" this chapter discusses can apply not only to possessions but also to practices. You can simply have too much draining stuff to do. What are the routine practices in your life that leave you dispirited? Why do you find them so? Are there any you can change?
2. Reflecting more on the "Why?" is important. For there are many reasons, our run-of-the-mill routines can sap our energy. Is it because a particular item on your "To Do" list is boring? Unpleasant? Tiring? Beneath you?
3. The essay notes that we "construct" the details in our lives. This construction often involves thinking of them as having diminished importance, meaning, or significance. Something in my life becomes a "detail" when I'd really rather be doing something else. If you find yourself dispirited by your mundane routines, what is your something else?
4. But this essay also suggests that if we can construct the details in our lives, we can also "reconstruct" them. Are you able to look at the details in your life in a different way? When I was a student, I had a job painting houses. Initially, I tolerated the routines of this job for the money, nothing more. But as the job went on, I developed an appreciation of the ready and well-demarcated progress possible in painting a house. While I regularly struggled with many of the more complicated problems in my life, I found an unexpected pleasure in the revitalized beauty of a newly painted residence.
5. In your own life, what would it entail for you to "honor" all your activities? Even activities that are unpaid? Unappreciated? Those that lack prestige? Activities whose value is uncertain or resides far off in the future?

6. Would you like to be Donnie, appreciating what others might regard as inconsequential? If not always, at least for moments in your life?

***

I've always liked the poet Robert Frost's line: "Home is the place where, when you have to go there, they have to take you in." "Home," in all the various ways we understand it, is clearly a place with rich connections and often deeply emotional moral tilts. The essay below considers home in the process of moving.

Home

I've been moving a lot lately. My new marriage has meant selling two homes and looking to buy a third.

Going through these moves with my wife, Hedi, reminds me that marriage isn't something I've simply added to my life, a new accessory that leaves my previously single life intact. Rather, marriage has a deeper impact. When it's working, it changes things completely. Bringing two dynamic lives together means each will unsettle the other in ways that can never be fully anticipated or predicted. On our first date, I was thinking about kissing her, not about selling houses. Yet here we are – a little over a year later – packing boxes and calling movers.

With all the moving, the everyday order I'd become attached to in my single years has disappeared. I can't find the simplest things – keys, wallet, toothbrush, underwear. Nothing is in the place my habits established for it.

I'm also astonished to find out how much I've accumulated while on my own. Going through the items in my attic and closets, I wonder why I've kept so many of them for so long. So, I've been throwing away things, giving away things, putting the rest in boxes.

In the temporary apartment in which we are staying while we look for a new home, I leave many of the boxes unopened. Moving reveals the true necessities of everyday life. I learn what matters to me by observing my willingness to spend time hunting for it, finding the right box, tearing off the tape, going through the wrappings. More things than I imagined aren't worth the effort.

I am coming to admire my Mom's philosophy of moving: When you move in, put everything into the cellar. Take things out of the cellar only when you're going to use them. After a year, give away everything left in the cellar. These are the things you don't really need.

Marriage has a way of teaching you the parts of your previously single self that you don't really need. As Hedi and I grow closer, I don't really need the part of me that had to be right. I don't really need the part of me that always had to do things a particular way. I don't really need the part of me that had to have his say.

Seeing me struggling with the hassles of moving, a real estate friend of mine reminds me: You're dealing with ordinary people in an extraordinary situation. This helps me keep things in perspective. Just as I was the day of my wedding, I am on edge during these moves.

And in a way this edginess is understandable. Whether it's doing a move or entering a marriage, transitions are vulnerable times. Things are easily broken in the process. During our moving, we lost a few glasses, but our relationship grew stronger. On both fronts, we count ourselves lucky.

As we look for a new place, I am for the first time in years not the owner of a house. There is no piece of real estate that I out of unconscious habit call mine. This thought occurs: If I no longer own a house, where is my home?

That, I suppose, depends in large measure on what I conceive of a home to be. Nestled temporarily in a comfortable apartment, this could be my home. It is pleasant enough. It even has amenities – a pool, a clubhouse, a walking path – our more permanent residences lacked. I love the breezes that blow through its grounds.

But moving reshuffles your life in interesting ways. To begin with, it gives you a new relation to the things you own. Even the items you cherish become burdens as you calculate the logistics of their storage or transport. We struggled for hours over what to do with our baby grand piano.

More deeply, moving transforms your relation to a place. As where you are becomes where you were, a subtle recalculation of your vacated domicile occurs. Some of what you valued, you are now ready to let go of. Having left her corporate job and started her own consulting firm, my wife was ready to leave a place where everyone is trying to get ahead of everyone else. Some of what you had to settle for is no longer a necessity. I won't miss my long commute and the rush hour traffic.

Most fundamentally, leaving a house can help you to redefine what a home is. My wife and I will miss parts of where we used to live. I'll miss the way my backyard overlooked a farm. She'll miss mornings on her sun porch. But in the midst of my current moves, I find that when I consider where I am, I think less of physical locales than the intricacy of a relationship. Home thus becomes less about a place and more about a person.

For me now, home is where Hedi is. I have a feeling it's my best move yet.

Personal Reflection Prompts

1. Where do you think of as "home"? Why? Wherever you think of as home, what makes it so for you? Try to list in your mind the key characteristics that give this place the quality of home for you.
2. Can you imagine a different kind of "home" for yourself? How would it differ from your present sense of your home? Is there something in your

imagination that your current home lacks? What would that be? Could you find it elsewhere?
3. Has your understanding of "home" changed over the years? How did you conceive of it then? How do you conceive of it now? The essay speaks of home as less about "physical locales than the intricacy of a relationship." Can a person determine where your home is?
4. Certainly, not all homes are supportive, welcoming places. Have you ever been in a home whose moral tilts were destructive?
5. Is part of the maturation of a person, the ability to leave home? More and more young people are delaying leaving home or returning to home after initially departing. Can home be an impediment to personal growth? A colleague of mine speaks of achieving "escape velocity" from his hometown as being for him an important professional move.
6. But as you pursue your professional goals with education and travel, can you lose your home? Must your gain necessarily involve a loss? Or conversely, to the degree your home made you the person that you are, can you take your home wherever you go?

***

This essay picks up on the chapter's suggestion that not all of our possessions are material in nature. It explores how some of our possessions that lack a physical reality may be among our most important.

Self-image

One of your most valuable possessions is something you might not even recognize as a possession. Yet it's with you almost constantly.

It's at least as close to you as your wallet, your car, your house. It's as intimately attached as that ring on your finger or the bracelet you never take off.

This precious possession I'm talking about is your self-image.

Your self-image is not your reputation. Your reputation is how others see you. Your self-image stems from your own inward gaze, how you stack up in your own eyes. Reputations are certainly important. They can mean getting that job, making that deal, gaining the trust of those around you. But your self-image is more deeply rooted. It will affect how you feel if you don't get that job, make that deal, or lose the trust of those around you.

At its most profound, this intimate possession can build you up or break you. That's why it's one of your most valuable possessions.

Your self-image is something others can easily damage. There are parents who withhold their love or dole it out sparingly or attached to too many conditions.

There are peers who mock or bully anyone who is different. There are colleagues who are quick to criticize your views or disparage your accomplishments.

All these exterior voices are at their most insidious when they over time begin to become your own. Internalize them all and you become your most intimate antagonist.

But distortions of your own making can also damage this precious possession. Such self-inflicted harm can occur, for instance, if you develop an inflated sense of yourself, when you become, as my wife likes to say, "full of yourself." Vain, conceited, haughty, self-regarding, egotistical. We have so many words for it because it's so widespread.

Here you can become your own worst enemy.

I've certainly been, at times in my life, my most intimate antagonist, and, at other times, my own worst enemy. Indeed, these two comportments have a way of becoming intertwined. It's when I'm most self-doubting that I'm inclined to subtly insert my own accomplishments into the conversation. It when I'm feeling insecure that my pronouncements tend toward the categorical, failing to consider nuance or qualification.

Untangling this psychological knot is not for the faint-hearted.

Consider, for instance, how you handle the criticisms by others that inevitably come your way. It's important to listen to them carefully, but not take them conclusively. They are, as one of my entrepreneur friends helpfully says, simply information. Take them in, process them. The key moment is what comes next.

This is because information by itself does not constitute meaning. The criticisms conveyed are merely the stuff out of which meaning can be made.

The criticisms are not you. Rather, you are how you respond to them.

Thus, while information is not by itself meaningful, it is in your hands always meaningful. It can help you figure out how not to become "full of yourself." It can save you from becoming your own worst enemy.

But be on guard against criticisms most insidious turn. That's their tendency to enable other voices to replace your own. Always remember your self-image belongs to you.

With something this valuable, how do you protect it? Even the most high-priced home security system is beside the point.

In processing the criticisms that come your way, it helps to consider the source. Every comment directed toward you is revealing something about the speaker.

A constant stream of criticisms betrays one motivation. The occasional critique amid a larger general comportment of affirmation another. A regular focus on minor slip-ups hints at one agenda. Reserving for life's pivotal moments the assertion of an uncomfortable truth reflects a different underlying purpose.

The stance I strive for is to be securely vulnerable, ready to be wrong, yet not believing it's a foregone conclusion. As I've gotten older, I've discovered

I've developed a strength in this kind of vulnerability. There's an increasingly deeper well of experience I can draw upon. Remembering the times I've been right can enable me to admit that this time I'm wrong. Having a record of accomplishments fosters a willingness to concede my present failure.

And always to realize: You're entitled to a bit of grace here. With the people that matter, you'll have the time to get it right.

Personal Reflection Prompts

1. Have you ever thought of your possessions as including more than the obvious tangible items? As this essay explores, your self-image is certainly a possession. You can possess it and you can lose it. What other kinds of nonmaterial possessions are important to you? Your honesty? Your resilience? Your hopes? If you regard such possessions as valuable, what are you doing to protect them from loss? You make sure your insurance is up-to-date to protect your house. You use dual authorization to protect your financial accounts. What are you doing to protect your spiritual valuables?
2. Like me, have you ever been your "most intimate antagonist" or your "own worst enemy"?
3. What is the key to being "securely vulnerable"? Even though I've gotten better at it as I've grown older, I still don't think I've completely mastered it. Try to recall times when you were able to feel securely vulnerable. What enabled you to do so?
4. Perhaps surprisingly, the essay claims that information "does not constitute meaning." While we all seek to be informed, it is important not to give too much power to brute data. When we do, we are giving away power that more appropriately resides in ourselves. Consider a bit of information you recently learned. What are the different ways you might interpret it? Selfishly? Generously? Skeptically? Faithfully?
5. Is there a bit of "teleopathy" in the self-image you are invested in? An unbalanced pursuit of being right? An overconcern with appearance? An unchecked pursuit for the approval of others? Remember, in checking the teleopathy in your life, you don't have to do it on your own.

***

This is an essay that I couldn't have written a year ago. It thus reminds me how much AI is becoming part of our lives – and how quickly. It is a thing that has the capacity to be a possession, a practice, and a place all at once.

Artificial Intelligence

I'm looking at the tree outside my den window. Usually, when I look out upon this large, beautiful tree on my front lawn, it inevitably gives me a bit of pleasure.

But not today.

That's because today it's only serving as an unsuccessful distraction from the disembodied voice that's been droning on my cell phone for the last half hour. This electronic voice repeats with regularity something like, "All our representatives are busy helping other customers. Your call is important to us. It will be answered in the order received." I'm discovering how irritating monotony can be.

Even getting to this static point has been a challenge. I've been navigating the whims of an unfailingly polite yet unceasingly frustrating chatbot. I thought I'd be making a quick, minor change to a beneficiary in my financial portfolio.

I was wrong. It may have been minor, but it wasn't quick.

The options the chatbot gives me aren't the options I'm looking for. It offers option A or B, but the change I want to make is neither. I feel like it's carving up the world in a way that fails to respond to the question I'm asking or, even more fundamentally, blocks me from telling the story I want to tell.

What seems to take precedence is not what I need, but rather what the chatbot or, more precisely, what its inscrutable creators have chosen to design.

Of course, this is the world we live in now.

And it's one I've readily taken advantage of. ChatGPT for a literature review. NotebookLM to enliven a presentation.

But I'm also seeing how it's increasingly taking advantage of me.

It's a world of pre-given options, structured steps, calculated distractions, and unwelcome addictions.

I used to daydream following the logic of my imagination. Now, the algorithms of YouTube lead to my next association and then the next one after that. The videos presented are often interesting and I lazily click along, but I'm left with a nagging feeling that the choices are not my own.

That's the rub.

Too often, even in the progression of my own thinking, it feels like someone else is calling the shots.

Of course, the options presented are algorithmically forged to reflect me, or so we're told. But the more I ponder it, the more I don't recognize the "me" I'm encountering. It's more a screen shot of yesterday's "me" rather than the self I'm working on and developing. It's more ossified than aspirational.

It's a flat, uninspired me. I'm not surprised that "brain rot" is the Oxford Word of the Year for 2024.

To be sure, I know I'll continue to take advantage of this AI-infused world. I love the efficiencies it enables. I relish the connections I continue to make. I enjoy the whimsical impulses it allows. Thanks to my Net surfing and surprising to my twenty something daughter, I've become a fan of Billie Eilish.

But while I definitely want to be *in* this AI-infused world, I just as surely don't want to be *of* it. I'm keeping a critical perspective, careful to bracket its alluring environs. It's a tool that I won't allow to become tyrannical.

So, for the moment, I'm turning off my phone. As I'm still very much alive, the minor beneficiary change I intended to make can wait. There's more to being alive today than the monotonous irritation of a too repetitive voice.

I exhale deliberately, turning again to the light coming through my window. I'm going to take a long, slow, unimpeded look at the tree outside. The leaves are gradually falling, one at a time, as if each is waiting its turn. It's a rhythm of a different kind. At the moment, it seems like it reflects more the "me" I want to be.

To everything, there is a season.

Personal Reflection Prompts

1. This chapter on developing the virtue of an attentive eye aims at the expansion of our perception, both outward and inward. It wishes to both widen and deepen our awareness. Consider the ways AI has become part of your life. Has it expanded your perception in either way? Conversely, are there ways AI has contracted your perception?
2. In the essay, I momentarily lost the pleasure of the view outside my window while enduring an annoying chatbot. Are there instances in your life that you've found technology similarly annoying?
3. What are the ways AI has made your life more productive? More creative? More helpful to others?
4. Do you place any limits on your use of AI? What are these limits? Why do you impose them? In your interaction with your AI-enabled devices, do you ever feel like someone else is calling the shots?
5. Do you think we are ready for the ways AI is transforming our lives? What do you see coming? How should we prepare? As scientist and futurist Roy Amara noted, "We tend to overestimate the effect of a technology in the short run and underestimate the effect in the long run."
6. Does AI ever distract you from something you regard as important? Even if you wished otherwise?
7. This chapter argues for the discernment of purpose as a way of holding unwanted distractions at bay. How are you presently discerning the purposes in your life? What skills do you need to do this well? Is there a particular purpose that keeps your life on track? Do you share it with others?

5

Our Relationship with That Which Is Greater Than Ourselves

An Open Spirit

> *"We must accept finite disappointment, but never lose infinite hope."*
> Martin Luther King, Jr.

Your Self-transcending Nature

Getting Unstuck

Developing the virtue of an open spirit is all about getting unstuck. With such an aspiration, this virtue runs into some powerful psychological forces that push in the other direction. While we might not use the technical vocabulary for these psychic dynamics, we regularly succumb to them whenever we keep believing or doing something simply because it's the approach we've always taken. The first is belief perseverance. It "solidifies ideas when our explanations of why they might be true outlast the discrediting of evidence that inspired them." The second is confirmation bias, which "motivates our search for belief-confirming evidence." Taken together, they expose us to the perils of ossified outlooks.

Such perils are plentiful and varied. As we've seen with other psychological obstacles, they are much easier to recognize in others. You might have encountered it when your friend keeps refusing to leave a romantic relationship that's obviously all wrong for her. You may have seen it with a coworker who's convinced the only problem with your team's dynamics is someone else. You may have wrestled with it in a contentious conversation with a relative on the other side of a political controversy.

But seeing it in yourself is much more challenging. After all, who wants to be wrong? It's embarrassing and a blow to your ego. You could end up needing to confront something you'd rather avoid. Thus, it's not surprising we have these psychic defenses against this ever happening. And that these defenses often remain largely unconscious and hidden from view.

Yet we are capable of adopting a contrary stance. An open spirit reflects a personal aspiration to nurture an open disposition. This is one that allows you to maintain doubts alongside your beliefs. It permits questions accompanying any answers you might provisionally offer. You can even take a cue from novelist Fyodor Dostoevsky's belief that the very nature of your faith resides in your process of searching for it.

In Chapter 1, we noted the self-transcending nature of consciousness. Speaking this way may sound a bit airy or pretentious, but there is really nothing esoteric or mysterious about it. It simply means you are never reduced to the current incarnation of yourself. You are not an object but an active subject. And because for an active subject, there are ever-present possibilities, there is likewise always the potential for affirmations of hope.

Thus, you are never as stuck as it may first appear, and the world is always larger than it initially seems.

From the Problems *in* Your Life to the Purpose *of* Your Life

If your life is anything like mine, problems abound and with some regularity, you get stuck. Still, even in your most entangled and distracted moments, your self-transcending nature provides an essential openness that offers the potential to be otherwise. Developing the virtue of an open spirit entails fostering this essential openness that enables you to adopt a larger angle of vision in those challenging moments.

It is in connecting with something larger than yourself that you can discern your purpose. For your purpose arises in your relationship to a newly recognized or discovered capaciousness in your world. Such a newfound purpose came to a friend of mine, for example, when he became a parent. "I stopped being a kid," he told me, "when I had one." When his newborn son came into the world, he learned the world held more possibilities than he had previously imagined.

Discerning your purpose can also bring to the fore a markedly different understanding of your talents and abilities. From this larger angle of vision, they are no longer simply a private resource for your personal gratification and advancement. They are, in an important sense, gifts. For such a larger angle of vision can deepen and extend your sense of your life, renewing an appreciation of what it took to develop your capacities. I think of how my father helped me with the many physical moves during my student days, enabling me to pursue my education. As I've been lately hauling heavy boxes up to my daughter's college apartment, I think to myself, "Thanks, Dad." I'm learning how as the recipient of my father's commitment to helping me develop my capabilities, I can now be the bearer of such gifts going forward.

A person as impressive as physician and polymath Albert Schweitzer never saw his brilliance as destined for his benefit alone. "I don't know what your destiny will be, but one thing I know," he said, "the only ones among you who will be truly happy are those who have sought and found how to serve."

A Striking Quality of Consciousness

Like anything we are long accustomed to, our consciousness – our simple everyday awareness – is something we rarely consider in any deep or sustained way. Our consciousness just *is* – and that's all we typically ask of it.

But like the classic cartoon of fish being blissfully unaware of water, as we metaphorically swim immersed in our consciousness, we can easily miss its striking characteristics.

One such striking quality is that consciousness is always conscious *of* something. In this manner, it is always going beyond itself. In prosaic ways, we notice this immediately whenever we attend to consciousness's self-transcending nature. For instance, as I write this, I might become newly aware of my mismatched socks, an unfortunate peccadillo of mine.

But upon reflecting more deeply, this self-transcending nature of consciousness has more than a prosaic import. In fact, it grounds one of the more impressive aspects of our character. As we are active subjects deciding how to direct our attention, we are continually making choices, both large and small. Crucially, this means we are always in the process of becoming someone new. Christian writer C.S. Lewis emphasized the importance of this feature of our consciousness. "[E]very time you make a choice," he writes, "you are turning the central part of you, the part of you that chooses, into something a little different than what it was before."

Our self-transcending nature – our always going beyond ourselves – thus implicitly poses a question: Amid our plentitude of choices, what are we attending to? What, in other words, is that toward which we are ultimately transcending? Awareness of my mismatched socks hardly exhausts the potential of this aspect of my character.

Indeed, if always going beyond ourselves is part and parcel of our nature, it prompts a much deeper inquiry: As we look out on an expansive world, how do we understand that which is greater than ourselves?

Turning to Spirituality

In turning to the topic of spirituality, I must confess a certain measure of nervousness, a feeling that I am going beyond my competence. As a professional ethicist, I am neither a theologian nor one who has been particularly active in traditional religious institutions. But in another way, I can see I am someone who has to write about this topic. For as part of this undertaking of moral reflection, I have committed to telling my story in the hope of encouraging you to tell your own.

In telling my story, the narrative necessarily arises out of the features of my own personal experience. In some sense, of course, this experience is purely subjective. It is filtered through all my quirks, biases, and ill-founded assumptions. My aim here is not to establish some grand objective truth. As the story is my own, it will doubtless reflect my limitations.

But it must also in important ways transcend them. The success of our undertaking here depends on you as a reader being able to connect your experiences with my own. Thus, my focus will be on some basic spiritual needs we all might share. In a significant sense, you as a reader of this book are a coauthor. As I indicated at the start, I'm eager to see how well we can work together.

The approach I envision might be called pre-doctrinal. That is, it will have little to say about the doctrines of particular sects or the conflicts such doctrines engender. Rather, it is my intention to explore the deeper intuitions that give rise to a spiritual sensibility. My belief is that at a basic level, many religions draw in different ways from the same experiential sources. By inviting you to explore these sources through the particular experiences of your own life, I hope to encourage an ethical undertaking that brings us together for an ongoing conversation.

A focus on the experiential sources of spirituality provides a way that people of diverse doctrinal beliefs – even those lacking any theistic conception – may connect with and develop. It respects a fundamental need that undergirds this book: We each should start wherever we are.

That Which Is Greater Than Ourselves

Among our wobbly moments, as I noted at the start of our undertaking, the "transcendental domain of our lives" is crucial, potentially grounding "the renewal of all our other relationships." This seems true of those who hold traditional religious beliefs as well as those who subject such beliefs to scrutiny. C.S. Lewis emphasizes the essential role of transcendence. "The man," he writes, "who is contented to be only himself, and therefore less a self, is in prison."

For Lewis, this transcendence takes many forms, including reading as well as worship. "Literary experience," he continues, "heals the wound, without undermining the privilege, of individuality. ... [I]n reading great literature I become a thousand men and yet remain myself. Like the night sky in the Greek poem, I see with a myriad of eyes, but it is still I who see. Here, as in worship, ... I transcend myself; and am never more myself than when I do."

Extending Lewis's human-centered formulation, some contemporary understandings of transcendence embrace a spirituality that emphasizes a focus beyond an "anthropocentric view," pointing to the potent currency of such issues as climate change and the emergence of AI. Many individuals today are engaging or exploring transcendence in their lives through a focus on either the deep complexity and beauty of the natural world or the awe-inspiring advances of artificial intelligence. The transcendent possibilities of the natural world embody a view of nature as having an intrinsic value, independent of human preferences or aspirations, and thus entitled to ultimate respect. The transcendent possibilities of AI find contemporary expression in the fascination with the singularity and the potential of artificial agents to gain intelligence and capabilities beyond our scope and understanding.

The scope of your spirituality is in the contours of your connection with something beyond yourself. It could be your family. It could be the common good of humankind. It could be the self-transcendence embodied in your political commitments or in your personal advocacy for social changes. Ideals of all types are a form of transcendence whenever they implicitly recognize a gap between the world as it is and the world as one believes it should be.

Thus, we can engage transcendence in an inclusive manner, akin to the way those in Alcoholics Anonymous do, all committing to depending on a "higher power," which they may understand in different ways.

Engaging Spirituality Together

As self-transcending beings, we are always connecting with something beyond ourselves. But what is this "something"? As a deep and integral part of an experience we all in some way share, this transcending quality of our lives is an undeniably rich one. For purposes of our reflective undertaking here, I encourage you to interpret it in whatever manner is most profoundly meaningful for you.

Thus, when I speak of God in touching upon the transcendental aspects of my own experience, I welcome you substituting whatever language or understandings best reflect your own personal beliefs or commitments.

First-person Spiritual Experiences

One reoccurring theme around a variety of spiritual experiences is an emphasis on the need to experience these engagements directly. Spiritual experiences have an essential lived-through character, difficult to understand by those lacking the particular experience. For instance, when listening to the emotional highs of world-class surfers, I feel I'm never fully grasping the heightened awareness they describe as their wave crests.

So, let's turn to a collection of first-person accounts. I've chosen a spectrum of individuals, each with some measure of public renown, so that you might also draw upon your wider knowledge of them. They are scientist Jane Goodall, singer and songwriter Paul Simon, television host Oprah Winfrey, and astronaut Edgar Mitchell.

Jane Goodall, Scientist

Jane Goodall is an English primatologist, famous for her groundbreaking work in studying chimpanzees. She would regularly immerse herself in their natural habitats. Deeply engaged in her observations, she recalls a moment when "I and the chimpanzees, the earth and trees and air, seemed to merge …"

Of that encounter, she says, "That afternoon, it had been as though an unseen hand had drawn back a curtain and, for the briefest moment, I had seen through such a window. In a flash of 'outsight' I had known timelessness and quiet ecstasy, sensed a truth of which mainstream science is merely a small fraction."

Paul Simon, Singer/Songwriter

In his songwriting process, Paul Simon speaks of experiencing something larger than himself in his creative moments. He says, "[S]ometimes you get plugged into a big, big force and you're a conduit – that's how it feels like. It's nothing to brag about; it's something to be grateful for."

The experience is for him an unexpected and overwhelming one: "Well, you never know when you're going to feel it. In my experience it's not a common occurrence, but there have been times when I've written a line that I had no idea I was about to write that just made me stop and lose my breath or cry. And I didn't know why, and I don't mean to say this as if I'm bragging about how good it was because most of the time I really thought, 'how did that happen?'"

Oprah Winfrey, TV Host

An American media mogul, best known for her widely successful talk show, Oprah Winfrey encountered her spiritual moment far from the noise of our contemporary media environment. She was hiking with a friend, and they suddenly stopped, taken in by the quiet.

As she describes the encounter: "'It' was the sound of silence. Utter and complete stillness. So still I could hear my own heart beating. I wanted to hold my breath, because even inhaling and exhaling was like a cacophony. There was absolutely no movement, no breeze, no recognition of air, even; it was the sound of nothing and everything."

And the effect on her is profound: "This was the most peaceful, coherent, knowledgeable moment I've ever witnessed."

Edgar Mitchell, Astronaut

As an astronaut, Edgar Mitchell encountered a vista few of us have experienced directly, viewing Earth from space. Encountering this larger vision, he says, left him with "an overwhelming sense of universal connectedness" and an abiding conviction of "the universe as in some way conscious."

The Misguided Attempt for Clear and Distinct Ideas, or Why Descartes Was Wrong

Knowing Ourselves as Subjects

The dynamic nature of consciousness is the locus of spirituality. For at the heart of our spiritual nature is our status as active subjects rather than objects. As active subjects, we are self-transcending beings. As our self-understanding changes, so does who we are. There is thus an essential openness to our character. And because of this, there are always affirmative possibilities before us. We can never, as Martin Luther King said, "lose infinite hope."

Living Our Lives as Objects

Yet, strange as it may initially seem, infinite hope is something we can have difficulty accepting. Why is this so?

It is in part because it takes from us the tempting comfort of resignation. There is a transient ease to giving up. If things can't possibly get better, why try? As one of my colleagues advised me during a particularly tense political conflict at work: "Jeff, just surrender." I must admit that at the time, his advice had its appeal. For once you give up, you are relieved of responsibility.

But while tempting, this sort of resignation is ultimately unsatisfying. Whatever the challenges or conflicts may be, they do not then simply go away. They reside in an ongoing and unstable dynamic of tension. And living with this dynamic of tension has its own kinds of psychic costs, from a loss of a night's sleep to a longer gradual erosion of your ideals.

Illusive Certainty

Amid our wobbly moments, we may be tempted by a "quest for certainty," as philosopher John Dewey once put it. Yet this too has its drawbacks we shouldn't ignore. For such a quest inevitably entails ignoring ourselves as active subjects and treating our lives as objects.

We treat our lives as objects whenever we attempt to explicate them exhaustively, to render them totally transparent. Under this approach, we seek serenity through certainty. Nothing is feared because everything is known.

At the start of our undertaking, we saw how with the self, we can never do this perfectly. This is because whenever you try to envision a fully explicit picture of yourself, rendering as transparent as possible all your features and subtleties, what inevitably escapes such attempts is the part of you that *perceives* this picture. You may, of course, then focus on the part of yourself doing the perceiving, but this would only lead to an infinite regress. The part of yourself perceiving your perceiving escapes your self-conception. As such, this can go on indefinitely. Because consciousness is by its very nature self-transcending, it can never be rendered totally transparent. The part of yourself rendering the rest of you transparent necessarily remains mysterious. You can never, in a word, capture yourself as an object.

What is true of yourself is also true of your engagement with your larger life. As a practical matter, total transparency in your larger life is elusive. It thus rarely can deliver certainty's hoped-for composure. Remember, you need fear nothing only after you know everything. But getting to know everything is exhausting, even with circumscribed projects. Consider, for example, something as simple as planning a family vacation. Bringing to awareness and giving careful consideration to all of the details – from hotels to expenses to care of the family dog while away – can be daunting. And given the supposed end of the vacation, somewhat counterproductive. Ever notice how the week before your vacation is always one of the most harried?

In his *Principles of Philosophy*, philosopher Rene Descartes wrote:

> "I call 'clear' that perception which is present and manifest to an attentive mind: just as we say that we clearly see those things which are present to our intent eye and act upon it sufficiently strongly and manifestly. On the other hand, I call 'distinct,' that perception which, while clear, is so separated and delineated from all others that it contains absolutely nothing except what is clear."

But in the ongoing unfolding of our larger lives, such a clarity and distinctiveness is hardly comprehensive. Seeking it too comes with its own debilitating circumscription. I am reminded of the classic story of a passerby noticing a man searching intently under the light of a street lamp. When the passerby inquired as to what the man was doing, the man said, "Looking for the watch that I lost." "Oh," replied the passerby, "Did you lose it on this corner?" "No," said the man, "I was walking on the other side of the street." Puzzled, the passerby asked, "Then, why are you looking for it on this corner?" Pointing to the street lamp, the man said, "This is where the light is."

If we only look at the parts of ourselves and the aspects of our world that are readily manifest or easily expressed, we will miss much of life, including its deeper and most satisfying moments. An inescapable aspect of moral exploration and reflection is that it will be frustratingly free of mathematical precision, supplying more pointers than proofs, much as we might prefer otherwise. Particularly with our most important and meaningful choices, there will always be "fear and trembling," as philosopher Soren Kierkegaard put it. Able to value only the clear and distinct knowledge of Descartes, we may remain metaphorically under the street lamp, missing all of the more expansive world beyond it.

Pointers, Intimations, and the Ineffable in Our Lives

Articulating the Ineffable

In his book *The Varieties of Religious Experience,* William James explored the character of our spiritual impulses, highlighting their ineffable quality.

According to James, such spiritual experiences are nonetheless profound. They can provide knowledge or perspective that is not accessible in a more discursive manner, such as Jane Goodall recounted in her experience, saying she "sensed a truth of which mainstream science is merely a fraction."

Along with their ineffable quality, these spiritual experiences also have a fleeting nature. As such experiences are transient, they can't be evoked at will or replicated upon demand. They are not under an individual's conscious control. Oprah Winfrey's encounter occurred in an unexpected moment, particularly for a talk show host: It was, she said, "the sound of silence."

Notably too, individuals undergoing spiritual experiences typically understand themselves as recipients, rather than sources, of such experiences. Paul Simon said of his writing of *Bridge Over Troubled Water*, "[I] hadn't really thought about how sometimes you get plugged into a big, big force and you're a conduit – that's how it feels like. It's nothing to brag about; it's something to be grateful for."

People also regularly report a strong sense of unity and connection in such experiences. Upon viewing the Earth from space, the astronaut Edgar Mitchell spoke of "an overwhelming sense of universal connectedness." Oprah Winfrey went on to affirm this powerful sense of oneness: "It felt like all life ... and death ... and beyond contained in one space, and I was not just standing it. I was also part of it."

These experiences often occur when someone has taken a step back from the hustle and bustle of their lives as occurred with TV host Winfrey. But these occasions of withdrawal from the world, offering a pause for reflection, hardly foster a passivity over a longer term.

They are, in fact, quite energizing upon reengagement with the world. Jane Goodall says that even though "imperfectly remembered," her experience supplied: "A source of strength on which I could draw when life seemed harsh or cruel or desperate." It was fundamentally empowering.

Tellingly too, the pervasive power of such experiences across a diversity of individuals springs from their openness to interpretation. Like the experience of rereading a good poem, the meaning of spiritual experiences can deepen and evolve. Such openness is not a deficiency but a positive defining feature, a continuing source to draw upon, like a well that never runs dry.

The virtue of an open spirit asks that we respect this open-ended and evolving quality of spiritual experience. When speaking of his inspiration during his songwriting process, Paul Simon says, "[I] don't want to go the next step and say that I think that bigger force is God. Nor do I want to say it's not. But I do want to recognize that there are times when something comes to you and you don't know why ..."

Developing the virtue of an open spirit entails respecting and engaging the many ways in which your responses to life's expansive complexities will at some level be partial or incomplete. It means accepting the unfinished quality of your own existence. Like Paul Simon, things will come to you, and you won't "know why."

Poetic Language

Understood in this way, spirituality is part and parcel of our nature, a constitutive dimension of ourselves. Yet it is something too easily overlooked or marginalized amid the practical demands and anxieties of our lives. As I well know, transcendence can feel frustratingly out of reach when you are late for your next business meeting or your daughter forgot her permission slip for today's school outing.

Still, it is crucial to always bear in mind the cost of losing the spiritual awareness that is an integral part of who we are.

The poignant words of the poet William Wordsworth provide a haunting reminder:

> There was a time when meadow, grove, and stream,
> The earth, and every common sight,
> To me did seem
> Apparelled in celestial light,
> The glory and the freshness of a dream.
> It is not now as it hath been of yore;—
> Turn wheresoe'er I may,
> By night or day.

The things which I have seen I now can see no more.

A Personal Peace that Surpasses My Understanding

As I said at the start of our undertaking, I am telling my story in a way that includes "the less secure, more fallible me." In providing "this more intimate portrait," I hope to encourage "a reciprocity of spirit" as you craft your own story. It is with this hope in mind, I feel I owe you a glimpse into my personal spiritual experience.

At the core of my spiritual experience is a profound peace that I wouldn't claim to fully understand.

The God I know grants me peace. Even during turbulent times, I can stop, take a breath, and feel it. This peace is more than an ordinary rest. When I stop to attend to it, this serenity in my life discloses a special character. It is a peace that reveals its *essential* nature. I experience this serenity in my life as something I cannot do without.

The essential character of this inner peace puzzles me. Why precisely do I experience it as something I can't do without? At first glance, the world appears to offer so much more. There are many things in the world that excite or attract me, so much so that I want them or at least think I do: money, recognition, influence, relationships. I expend considerable energy seeking these things. Surely, if I obtain even some of them, life can be good.

Yet my experience of this peace as essential exists. Why?

It seems to me important to consider the manner in which I can *have* the many other things I want if I am fortunate enough to obtain them. I cannot have them as things in themselves. I can only have them as they exist for me. My use or enjoyment of them is necessarily filtered through my own consciousness.

Thus, the pleasure I derive from these objects of my desire is inevitably conditioned by the person I am. Money, we are often told, cannot buy happiness. We regard this as a truism but seldom examine the reason why. It is true because whatever value money has for us depends on the meaning we attach to it. Money itself can't bring happiness because by itself it is only half the equation. Whether or not money brings us happiness depends on the significance we bring to money.

If I lack an inner serenity, I will bring to all the world offers me this particular form of self-deficiency. This deficiency will affect the character of my desires, helping to shape the value of each object for me. The value of each object will come to lie in how it addresses this gap in myself. The danger here is that of using an external good to address an internal need. This confusion obscures the genuine good of the object – what money, for instance, can actually provide – and creates alluring but illusive possibilities – what money can only appear to provide.

Let's stay with the example of money, exploring the dynamics of its illusive possibilities. The money we have changes the way people treat us. A cab stops and picks us up only because the driver expects we have the money to pay for the ride we request. A waiter strives to provide good service, knowing that if we have the resources to dine at an elegant restaurant, we have the power to reward him handsomely.

But money also changes the way people treat us in more subtle and complex ways. I recall a while ago meeting a wealthy executive. I was struck by the way he *expected* people to listen to him. He was used to having people's attention when he spoke. Such an expectation, I imagine, develops in a workplace environment dealing with individuals whose careers and livelihoods you control.

Let's suppose that for whatever deeper psychological reasons, this executive has an insecure streak, that he struggles in his feelings of self-worth. Many ostensibly successful people I know (I should probably include myself here) have this makeup. Indeed, it is often one of the roots of their success. External achievement is one of the ways we deal with internal struggle.

Now, I had noted earlier how a lack of inner security colors my use or enjoyment of the objects I desire. Generally speaking, the value of objects for me arises from how they address my particular form of restlessness. Now, the executive's particular form of restlessness, which we are supposing, consists in a basic insecurity. This necessarily becomes part of the significance he brings to his money.

Money changes the way people treat him. People *attend* to him in a special way. This special attention is a basic attribution of value. It carries with it an external recognition of the business leader's self-worth.

Such external recognition thus can be the way his money addresses the particular gap in himself. On the assumptions we are making, the meaning he brings to money is an affirmation of self-worth.

Carrying this significance, however, money becomes an external substitute for an internal need. In this way, money's genuine good is obscured by an illusive possibility. Money can add to your bank account, but it can't increase your fundamental self-worth. The worth of the self must be determined by the self, not the objects at its disposal. While the executive might enjoy the special attention he regularly receives from others, indeed over time might even acquire a compulsive need for such attention, such an illusionary pursuit leaves the underlying psychological dynamic unattended. He might well come to need money more and more, and continue to acquire it. But his more fundamental need remains unmet.

All this illustrates what the world can offer to someone who is not at peace. It can obscure the genuine value of goods, such as money, and elevate their illusionary appearances. Obscuring the genuine value of goods is dangerous to your needs. Elevating the illusionary appearance of goods is dangerous to your aspirations.

Both these possibilities leave your underlying restlessness unattended. In my life, it is the peace that surpasses my understanding that provides the antidote to this all-too-human malady. It's an abiding experience of which I've never attempted a greater explanation. The soul, as Emerson says, "never reasons, never proofs, it simply perceives." And in many ways, that is enough.

Wisdom for an Open Spirit

The virtue of an open spirit arises out of your self-transcending nature. Your consciousness is always conscious *of* something, whatever more expansive horizon or context constitutes your world. As an active subject, you are never stuck in any permanent existential way because by your very nature you are always reaching beyond yourself. This also means your world is always larger than it may at any point initially appear. This is because in reaching beyond yourself, you are continuingly exercising the potential to imbue new meanings in the possibilities emerging in your world. The only fundamental question concerns the choices you are making. And given the self-transcending creatures we are, there is always another question that can follow any answer you might provisionally give in making your choices.

Wisdom for an open spirit is thus the kind of wisdom that Socrates claimed. Human wisdom for him stemmed from knowing what he did not know. It meant embracing an intellectual humility. Developing the virtue of an open spirit entails adopting a posture in your life of curiosity and inquiry. It involves a welcoming engagement of conversation with others, testing your assumptions and beliefs. It means an ongoing commitment to self-reflection and an eagerness to learn. In developing an open spirit, doubt can deepen faith, rather than undermining it.

Discerning Purpose

Such an ongoing and open engagement with your world brings to the fore the question of purpose. For discernment of your purpose is simply a recognizing of the relationship you are claiming to your world. It is your commitment to something larger than yourself, however you might conceive of it. As we saw earlier, it can have a galvanizing effect on college students pursuing their education, enriching their intellectual development, increasing their community involvement, and promoting a focus on their larger life aims.

In Chapter 4, we considered the opposing risks of a misfocused and an unfocused comportment in your life, each in its own way unsettling the wholesome balance of a properly focused attention.

In coming to understand your purpose, there is no mechanical test here, no algorithm you can employ. Rather, such a pursuit calls for human judgment and discernment. It thus of necessity entails a certain measure of uncertainty and a willingness to reevaluate as your life goes forward. It is as much a process as a result.

Still, there are some touchstones that can guide you – and these are touchstones that the virtues you have been developing can provide.

A purpose is something to which you can wholeheartedly give yourself. It doesn't allow for a divided self. It is not an enervating source of internal division or tension. On the contrary, a purpose as I mean it here is fundamentally self-nourishing. It calls on multiple parts of yourself to coordinate and mutually reinforce each other. In this way, the pursuit of purpose draws upon the virtue of a holistic mind.

The pursuit of purpose also draws upon the virtue of an empathetic heart. As your pursuit of purpose defines your relationship to your world, it necessarily contemplates the others who share your world, including their needs. It can never be merely solipsistic. It doesn't deplete, it augments. It fosters growth and extension.

In defining your relationship to your world, your purpose must further attend to the things in your world. In this, it draws upon an attentive eye. Such an intellectual and sensory awareness can help to shape your pursuit of purpose, influencing it strategies and choices. For a critical part of discerning your purpose is recognizing how to best implement it. This requires a probing and intimate knowledge of the environments you will need to navigate.

Yet the preeminent virtue for the pursuit of purpose is that of an open spirit. For an open spirit is the virtue that focuses most fully and expansively on what is larger than yourself. And in fostering a posture of skepticism toward received wisdom, this virtue encourages your pursuit of insights that bear the distinctive imprint of your character. It opens up for you a life you can personally affirm. It's your way, as Steve Jobs liked to say, of putting your dent in the universe.

I recall how my own developing discernment of purpose evolved during my college years. It came in fits and starts, but solidified in the way I framed my core identity during my later 20s and early 30s. It was – and is – a commitment to the twin values of seeking and service.

My penchant for seeking surfaced early on; I often remember how, to my father's annoyance, I endlessly peppered him with questions as he was trying to concentrate while driving. Now, at this point, my desire to understand the world around me is something I doubt I could jettison, even if I wished to do so. While the topics that spark my curiosity have evolved considerably over the years, this basic inquiring spirit abides as part of my identity.

That said, seeking by itself always felt oddly incomplete, as if its isolation deprived it of its fuller meaning. The famous analogy of Plato's cave captivated me as an undergraduate, as I followed its progressive understanding of reality from the illusion of the shadows to the illumination of the sun. I remember reading *The Republic* for the first time and having trouble catching my breath, as I was transported by the power of its philosophic vision.

For Plato, the cave's interior represented the everyday, physical world perceived by our senses, and the cave's exterior represented the intellectual realm accessible through our reason and philosophic reflection.

Captivating though I am by this intellectual realm, I spend much of my life today within the quotidian virtues of the cave's interior, tapping the everyday opportunities for outreach it engenders. Even during my college years, I would regularly abandon the library for community service, taking low-income kids from the city on field trips, for instance, or volunteering at a nearby halfway house. I needed to know the difference my breathless philosophic sojourns might make to the lives of those around me.

Who you are always has a transcendent dimension, something that can neither be fully captured nor exhausted by the challenges of your professional life, providing a lodestar even in the most turbulent of times. For me, this lodestar is a double commitment to seeking and service. Yours will be different and distinct, of course. But the important thing, I've found, is to regularly embed and nurture this dimension in your daily actions.

Set against being misfocused or unfocused is your aspirational pursuit of purpose. A misfocused stance is a distortion of your life. For me, that would have been remaining aloof in the alluring, yet airy, abstractions outside Plato's cave. An unfocused stance is a distraction from your life. For me, that occurs whenever I neglect the importance of reflecting upon and questioning why I do what I do. You'll know you're on the right path in pursuing your purpose when it both integrates and elevates your life.

Virtues as Gifts

In William Sullivan's *Liberal Learning as a Quest for Purpose*, he emphasizes how bringing the question of purpose to the fore can reframe our personal abilities. "It was important, however, that personal abilities were reframed within the vocational narrative. From being personal assets, they came to be talked about as 'gifts' for which the individual should be grateful, but about which the right question was how these gifts might be developed and employed."

Such a reframing points the way to the organic relationship between virtues and purpose, once such virtues are properly understood. The four virtues at whose development the book aims are certainly "personal assets," but that is not all they are. Like all our individual talents and potentials, they are also "gifts" of which we can rightly ask "how these gifts might be developed and employed."

"Drives" and "Callings"

Reconceiving the virtues as gifts points to a new way of understanding one's underlying motivations for engaging in ethical reflection and exploration. We can think of such motivations as "drives" or "callings." In discussing the educational value of discerning purpose, William Sullivan brings out this dynamic. "What difference might it make, for learning about purpose," Sullivan asks, "when educators speak of students as 'driven,' as contrasted with being 'called'?"

These differing metaphors give rise to strikingly different comportments in individuals. Framing our motivations as "drives" points inward. As Sullivan explains, "The drive metaphor draws attention to our 'passions' and what they move us toward, including how most effectively to obtain these things. In this perspective ideas are instruments, tools for attaining our desires."

Framing our motivations as "callings," however, fosters an outward orientation. "In contrast, call has a different metaphorical resonance. It focuses our attention outward, toward the larger world of relationships and connections. The metaphor of call highlights precisely what is neglected by the drive metaphor: our experience of living with others within a context characterized by values and relationships that attract us or to which we feel drawn to respond."

The calling metaphor for the virtue of an open spirit is especially apt. For, as the preeminent virtue for discerning purpose, this virtue "focuses our attention outward, toward the larger world of relationships and connections." It resists, as Sullivan would put it, "the apparently automatic quality of our desires and aversions." It contemplates that which is greater than ourselves.

So, are you "driven" or "called"?

Topical Reflections

This first essay is about finding spirituality in unexpected places. Has this ever happened to you? Because such spirituality may come in forms you don't anticipate, how would you recognize it?

Worship

On the way to church one Sunday, I see golfers on a roadside fairway. The course is a beautiful one, lush and green, extending off into the distance – an athletic Eden. They have their Sunday ritual just as I have mine.

The golfers have their studied strokes and practiced incantations, their pilgrimage from one green to the next. With each swing, there is a solemn hush, like the pause of a congregation before the raising of the chalice. Then, a transubstantiation occurs as the ball rising up is momentarily transformed into hope incarnate.

The great thing about the golf course, one golf enthusiast tells me, is that no one can reach you there. It is, from his worldly perspective, a secular sanctuary, a safe place to pause.

Worship for me also begins with a pause, a break from the demands of my daily routine. This necessary disengagement allows for a deeper reengagement.

When the utility of the world recedes, its simple wonder comes to the fore. Everything acquires a significance beyond itself.

My Sunday ritual differs visibly from the golfers,' to be sure. But such surface differences do not always matter. Any ritual worth its salt expresses something more. The distinctive value of a ritual occurs when it transcends its own external features, when its words deepen into silence. The essence of a ritual lies in its intimations.

I've been a churchgoer all my life – sometimes in organized groups, sometimes in solitude. Sometimes even in secret from myself. This variety in my religious experiences exposes an important truth: Seeing spiritual matters clearly involves dissolving form and revealing substance. It is when you are separated from the particularities of place that you discover how every person's self is a cathedral.

As a boy, I enjoyed miniature golf and begged to be taken often. (It may have helped my elementary-school ego that my frequent partner – the girl next door – had a mother who would warn her not to beat me.) In my adult years, I've rented a bucket of balls and worked out my tensions on the driving range. I've even braved a single lesson with a golfing pro. But only once have I played golf proper.

It was as a member of a wedding party. Trying to calm a nervous groom, we played the day before the ceremony on a local course. But even here my play would have troubled a true believer. Noisy and rowdy, unconcerned about my score, I broke more rules than I knew. Enjoying the heretical pleasure of sinning without guilt, I'm sure I offended more than a few.

But I would pause before playing this way again. Golf, after all, is a serious pursuit for many serious people. I've taken in the reverential tone of commentators, watched the joyful communion of players, seen the dedication to mastery of practice, and observed the faithfulness to the weekly celebration. I suspect there is more going on than meets my eye. And whenever this occurs, I've learned to pause – to speak less and listen more, heeding but not confronting the differences of others.

Spiritual differences are real, and such differences deserve our scrutiny. All persons are created equal, but all doctrines are not. Further, in the spiritual realm, mistakes are particularly profound. If we fail here, our successes elsewhere cannot help us.

But we must also appreciate the subtlety of success in this arena. What ultimately matters in the spiritual realm is not the character of the signs but the substance they signify. We grow when we look beyond the comfortable signs of our childhood.

So each Sunday I visit the services of a sect that is not my own, if only for the few moments that my car speeds by. They seem a friendly crowd that would welcome me if I chose to stop and linger. I have not yet grasped the mysteries of their liturgy but enjoy a sense that fellowship may someday be possible. In its own way, this expanse of green is clearly sacred ground for those who walk it. I know their visible signs and wonder how far their substance is from mine.

Personal Reflection Prompts

1. If the virtue of an open spirit is all about getting unstuck, you need to consider what are the factors that get you stuck. Remember the psychological dynamic of belief perseverance "solidifies ideas," giving them a weight that makes them hard to overcome, even when new evidence becomes available. Most of us don't like to change our minds. It too often involves a chipping away at our egos or least disrupts the confident, competent images we wish to project to others. But Nobel laureate Daniel Kahneman said, "Most people hate changing their minds, but I like to change my mind. It means I've learned something." This represents the ever-present ethos of the open spirit. When it comes to your spirituality, are you ready to learn something? Have you ever gained a new spiritual insight? How did it come about?
2. One of the ways we get stuck is by emphasizing form over substance. In this essay, I encountered a set of Sunday rituals different from my own. But I wondered what I'd see if I looked beyond the unfamiliar forms to what was going on beneath them. What would I come to understand if I saw the pastoral ritual of the Sunday golfers through their eyes? It's all too easy to miss an insight because it comes in an unexpected package. Have you ever learned something from a child or someone younger than you? Have you ever learned something from someone less experienced or educated or successful than you are?
3. Spiritual wisdom often has an ineffable dimension. Philosopher Ludwig Wittgenstein famously wrote, "Whereof one cannot speak, thereof one must be silent." Are there things you know that you can't easily find the words for? Are there things you're sure of even if you can't prove them to others? How do you react to such beliefs in others, especially if their beliefs seem to you to be erroneous or ill-founded? Do you grant them the respect you wish them to grant you?
4. As spiritual wisdom can be difficult to put into words, people often find spiritual understanding and connection in rituals. The golfers I observed certainly had their own distinctive rituals. Do you have any such rituals? How did you find them? Why do you think they work for you? Do you do them alone or with others? Has a ritual ever worked at one time for you but now no longer does? What happened?
5. Are there dangers in claiming an esoteric spiritual knowledge? In believing that you know or understand something better than others? How can you guard against spiritual self-deception?

***

This essay explores the value of something as apparently unproductive as sleep. In doing so, it brings into view another dimension of spirituality, that of struggle and surrender.

Sleep

The moment before falling asleep has a spiritual side to it. It is the still moment in the motion of my day. A time when I am reminded of my limits and place my struggles in the hands of others. When I sleep, I surrender.

The moment that occurs each night just before I slip from wakeful consciousness is delicious. My muscles relax, and I sink deeply into the mattress. My breathing slows, and there is a renewed awareness of sound and sensation. With my window open, I hear the familiar buzzing of insects and feel a cool breeze across my chest. The soft linen on my pillow cradles my cheek. I am at rest.

From a popular perspective, I suppose, I am doing nothing of value. We are suspicious of sleep nowadays. Busyness is in vogue.

Still, I like to sleep when I can, though I've had to get used to reprimands from friends. I recall a time when a friend called and awakened me in the late morning (OK, maybe it was a little after noon) and was incredulous to find me still in bed. He felt comfortable criticizing me as if I had broken a rule that everyone knows.

Later, I think: I should have told him I was only enacting my own version of the physician's creed ("First, do no harm"). It's hard to hurt anyone when you're under the covers.

There is nothing inherently admirable in busyness. It can stem from personal inadequacy or neurotic compulsion as well as the aim of accomplishment. Busy people don't always get the most done. Yet today busyness has a certain cache. Important people are busier than others. We tend to think we matter more when we don't have time to spare. A friend of mine thought there was some status jockeying when she asked her business colleague about their one o'clock meeting, and he retorted, "I have two meetings scheduled for one o'clock, and neither one is with you."

Idle hands may do the devil's work, but someone genuinely at rest is never idle. Idleness occurs only when there is an underlying restlessness. This is when untoward things can happen.

And remember: busyness has its own dangers. I think of this whenever I see someone speeding along the highway engrossed in talking on his car phone. I hope for my sake and his he is watching where he is going.

Of course, some people sleep for the wrong reasons. They sleep to escape. They are hiding from something uncomfortable, avoiding something too challenging. They are not genuinely at rest. Good sleep is something earned. (I feel about them the way an older colleague must have felt about me when he looked at me and said, "You're too young to be cynical.")

The best sleep occurs on the other side of accomplishment. It happens only after having met the challenge, when you're comfortable enough to let go, after you've grappled with complexity and discovered underneath it some serene and simple truth.

Occasionally, I'll pose a question in my class that I intentionally won't answer, and then invite students in the days that follow to attempt to answer the question on their own. A few days after having posed such a question, a tired-looking student came to me. Explaining that he'd been thinking about the question since class, he entreated me for the answer. "I keep thinking about it," he said, "and I can't sleep." Though sympathetic to the student's plight, I still consider it one of my finer teaching moments – when I was able to disturb a student's sleep.

In a way, I envy him the way he is just beginning the journey. In a way, I'd never go back.

This is because part of a good life is certainly accomplishment – there are things each of us need to do, ways we need to grow. Fail here, and life is not good. But part of a good life is a deeper remembering, a thankful recognition of what we already have. My life has many gifts. And I remember them, each night as I lie in bed and my muscles relax and my breathing slows and I am at rest.

Personal Reflection Prompts

1. When you settle into bed and drift off to sleep, are you doing nothing of value? Simply recovering so that you can once again fight whatever battles you encounter the next day? The essay ponders if something more is going on. What do you get in this time of respite from your daily activities? Do you ever see or feel things that you missed earlier in the day? Do you think you are learning things even while you sleep? Have you ever awakened with an important idea or realization that wasn't there the night before?
2. This essay sees the moments of falling asleep as when you place your "struggles in the hands of others." Do you ever put your struggles in the hands of others? Why or why not? Does it make you feel selfish? Less competent? Less in control? I had a colleague once tell me he rarely does so because he usually feels he is the person best equipped to handle most situations. Is that ever you? Conversely, is there something positive about needing other people? Is there a different type of strength or competence in acknowledging or admitting such a need?
3. The essay speaks of being reminded of your "limits." Why might such a reminder be important or significant? Recall a time when you were reminded of your limits. An occurrence when you didn't have enough time or the right skills or the requisite amount of patience. What was your reaction? How did

others react to your recognition of your limits? Did it go well? If not, how could you have handled it differently?
4. When are the times or occasions in which you feel genuinely at rest? Do they come often? Would you want more of them? Do they come when you are active? Idle? Around others? Alone?
5. Many individuals, as I did, report their version of spirituality as being a cure for restlessness. In Oprah Winfrey's account of her spiritual experience, she describes it as "most peaceful," a moment marked by "silence" and "stillness." Do you ever turn to something "greater than yourself" for moments of peace, silence, and stillness? How would you describe or explain "that which is greater than yourself" in such moments?

***

Because our thinking takes us beyond ourselves, it is pregnant with spiritual possibilities. But it can also get us off-track. The following essay explores the possibilities along with the pitfalls of thinking.

Thinking

People often tell me I think too much. I've heard this since I was a boy. I know I let some things bother me more than I should. A passing conversation that didn't go well. A possibly perturbed look from a colleague. Not getting to the thirty-seventh thing on my day's "To Do" list.

But when I think about it (See, here I go again!), I think that while folks who say I think too much are on to something, it's something different than they believe. It's not that I need to think less than I do. It's that I need to think better. The change I need lies in the quality, not the quantity, of my reflection.

We do not live in a thoughtful age. We live in one that worries a lot. In many ways, this anxiety is paradoxical. We worry more than our parents and grandparents even though they had more to worry about. By many objective standards, our lives are better than our elders. Food. Clothing. Health. Shelter. Education. Yet despite these improvements, we are less at ease.

We are so in part because of the quickened pace of our lives. Technology allows us to do more, and, by choice or necessity, we've tended to take advantage of it.

But it's not simply that we're doing more. We're doing more in a different way. Increasingly, our interactions outside the cyberworld tend to resemble those within it. The trend is toward simultaneity, toward a world where everything is available all at once. Not only does the internet break down barriers; So does

Walmart. We find our lawn chairs and groceries in the same aisle. We get an oil change while we fill our prescriptions.

As life moves at a faster clip and more is available to us at each moment, we of necessity think more. We do so of necessity because a world in transition renders our habits less reliable.

But while we think more, we also think more mundanely. Rather than examining the meaning of our work, we worry about making a client's deadline. We look for the best deal on a new cell phone, even as we fail to consider how we are communicating with our spouses. Rushing out each morning, we check our hair but not our character. Rather than reflect, we fret.

The upshot of these daily absorptions is this: Overwhelmed in our lives, we leave them underexamined.

Good thinking has a way of taking us beyond ourselves. We readily recognize this whenever we are transformed by the thought of a brilliant philosopher or an insightful poet. But we frequently miss the opportunities our own choices offer for self-transcendence.

Daily self-reflection helps us to recognize these opportunities. By making good thinking a part of our lives, it brings to our lives a transcendent character. For every time we think deeply about ourselves, we take a step beyond ourselves. We cross a boundary. We become something new.

Through promoting self-renewal, this habit of daily reflection can reveal to us a new depth to the world. For in becoming something new, we can connect with something more. In our ability to transcend ourselves, we can recognize something greater than ourselves.

At its best, daily self-reflection can open up that sacred space toward which our secular selves aspire. It can create a space for God.

Of course, you can't create this place in your life without clearing away the underbrush that's been accumulating. All those little everyday worries and anxieties that over time have taken root. It isn't easy, but it's worth the effort.

For my part, I'm going to try to worry less about getting to the end of my "To Do" list each day. I'm going to attempt to remember that possibly perturbed look of a colleague may come from what he had for lunch. I'm going to let some passing conversations just pass by.

These aims are worthy because they create the possibility of more worthy thoughts. I think better when I think about more than the immediately pressing parts of my life. Some days, struggling with the meaning of my work may be worth renegotiating a deadline. Sometimes, I should turn my cell phone off to better communicate with my wife. And in my rush out in the morning, I want to take a moment to think about my character before combing my hair.

And I want to remember: Properly done, every thought is as prayer.

Personal Reflection Prompts

1. Do you ever find yourself thinking too much? Consider for a moment when this tends to happen for you. What sets it off? How might you recognize when you are overthinking something? Do you have ways of reining in your overactive mind when this occurs? In my family, we call any sort of obsessive, unproductive, or misguided thinking by a name – "stinking thinking." Do you have persons in your life that you can turn to for helping to quell your stinking thinking moments? If not, how could you go about finding them?
2. Do you agree with this essay's contention that, "We do not live in a thoughtful age"? If you do, why is this so? With our cell phones' ready access to the internet's ever-expanding abundance of information, we have a multitude of sources that might inspire or provoke our thinking. Yet I spend more time than I'd like to admit with the many mindless amusements that same internet makes so easily available to me.
3. Throughout *Seeking Your Better Self*, we emphasized the role of the virtues – from a holistic mind to an open spirit – in enhancing the quality of your reflection. From your perspective, what are the characteristics of good thinking? Conversely, what do you see as the features of poor thinking? Can someone exhibit a high quality of thought even when arriving at conclusions to which you object? Could you name a person who does so? What features of their thinking do you appreciate or even admire?
4. What topics are worthy of your thought? By that, I mean what topics are most important or valuable for you to consider or reflect upon? You don't have the time, energy, and ability to think about everything, so you have to make choices. How are you choosing? Do you think you are choosing well?
5. What might it mean that when properly done, "every thought is a prayer"?

***

Interruptions also come with transformative spiritual insights. But in my own life, they're something I've long struggled with and not always welcomed. Is there a better way for us to understand the interruptions in our lives?

Interruptions

I'm not someone who's particularly good with interruptions. At work, I suppose, I've learned to handle them reasonably well. But even there I relish the early mornings before my phone starts buzzing.

It's not that I aspire to be, in the current lingo, a "multitasker." You can get too comfortable with doing too many things at once. I remember reading about a fellow who would always take out two adjacent phones at airports so he could retrieve his messages with one while at the same time making his calls with the other. I wouldn't want to be the fellow's son trying over the line to tell his busy dad what happened in school today.

But I've been noticing the way I invest in my plans, the way I judge the present out of my past expectations. The way I implicitly define the good life is as getting what I hoped for.

Interruptions, by definition, frustrate our current endeavors. They break the continuity of the task at hand. They take us from what we had chosen to do.

But they can also revise our perspectives. They can help us to see things in situations we didn't see before. A long line at the supermarket is an opportunity to enjoy the antics of the three-year-old in the cart ahead of you. A traffic jam is a chance to put your hand on your wife's arm and tell her that you love her.

Sometimes, if interruptions happen at the right moment, they can even cause us to look at ourselves anew. I've noticed how when I get interrupted, my aims and expectations get thrown into relief. Because they've been frustrated, I perceive them more clearly. And once they've crystalized, I do not always like what I see.

I'm a planner, no doubt. I always have been, to a fault. (The thought of losing my day planner still produces an involuntary tensing of my muscles.) But whatever success I've had in this regard, there's an underlying futility to my efforts. At 10, I didn't grasp my views at 20; at twenty, I didn't discern my outlook at 30, and so on. It's folly to think my wisdom of the present moment is any less mutable.

At bottom, this is the hubris in my planning: the way I assume the superiority of my present self. I can hold to it like a raft going over the rapids.

But life isn't all rapids. There are side pools and some clear stretches of water. Many times when you can safely let the raft go. Indeed, sometimes jumping from the raft is the only way to safety.

The fundamental virtue of interruptions is the way they point us to something beyond ourselves. Interruptions remind us that our goals aren't the only goals. They instruct us in life's more intimate politics, teaching daily the art of the possible.

For in every interruption, there is a need other than your own. I'm not the only one who hoped to pick up something quickly at the supermarket or who left early intending to avoid the Sunday evening traffic. In their insistent way, interruptions remind us of how we share the world with those around us.

I don't want to be the fellow with two phones in hand at the airport. He's trying to avoid the education a good interruption can provide, attempting to reduce the world to his needs.

I'd rather learn to recognize the hidden insights in the interruptions of my life. Attended to properly, they provide glimpses of the better self I seek.

You never know when hearing about a child's day at school could be just the education you need.

Personal Reflection Prompts

1. There is a spiritual side to interruptions. That's because of "the way they point us to something beyond ourselves," a feature this essay describes as a "virtue." In this sense, interruptions can be a valuable companion for developing an open spirit. But as the essay notes, they don't often feel that way, understandably so, because they tend to "frustrate our current endeavors." So, how do you handle interruptions? Are there ways in which you'd like to improve your responses to interruptions?
2. Interruptions also frustrate our desire for control – "They take us from what we had chosen to do." They impede us from calling the shots, at least in the way we had intended to do. But this can also be another side of spirituality – where something comes to us from the outside rather than arising from our own efforts, such as how Paul Simon describes the insights in his own songwriting. Was there a time when you gave up control and things turned out even better than you expected?
3. An open spirit takes aim at the perils of ossified outlooks. Did you ever encounter an interruption that helped you see things from a different perspective? Was it valuable? Have you ever tried to reframe your initial or habitual reaction to an interruption? Give it a try next time you're feeling frustrated or impatient. Were you able to see it with new eyes? Did you learn anything about yourself or someone else?
4. Did an interruption ever get you unstuck?
5. Flipping our discussion and looking at it from the other side, are there times that it's important, even crucial, that you are not interrupted? What are those times? What did you do to ensure you remained free of interruption? You should never be reluctant to assert your legitimate priorities. But a bit of planning helps. I think of my parents when we were young kids. They had a latch inside their bedroom door. Then, I never understood why. Now, I do.

***

Throughout my life, time has puzzled me. This has been the case both at a practical level and as a philosophic conundrum. Perhaps you too have in some way struggled with time? If so, knowing Einstein shared in this struggle, we can find comfort in that we are not alone.

Time

Time puzzles me. It puzzles me because I never seem to have enough.

Now, it may seem curious that I'm puzzled by my own lack of time. After all, I'm hardly alone in this regard. Being pressed for time is an all-too-common feature of contemporary life.

Still, my everyday hurriedness often gives me pause. This is because whenever I'm able to take a step back from a hectic day, I'm struck by the feeling that my overscheduled hours are other than they should be. I mean this not in a superficial sense – purchasing a top AI Calendar Assistant won't solve my problem – but in a much more fundamental way. If I'm always rushing, something feels cosmically out-of-whack.

The God I believe in created an ordered, purposeful universe, one that offers each of us a special calling. If He is calling us, He must have given us the time we require to heed His call. On this premise, I have all the time I really need.

Thus, I'm only moving too fast because I'm making mistakes. Doing the wrong things or doing the right things in the wrong way or doing things in the right way for the wrong reasons. The fundamental fault lies not in the nature of things, but in the nature of my choices.

For much of my professional life, my mistaken choice was being caught in a career rather than being true to a calling.

Now, at first glance, a calling may look like a career. Callings can carry with them many of the same external features. Titles. Salaries. Deadlines. But callings are fundamentally different than careers.

Careers arise out of the market. They spring from what's in demand. But a calling is more securely anchored. It resides within. It's the gift of a coincidence between your own development and the needs of others.

Teaching for me is a calling. Through it, I become who I am by helping those who sit in my classes discover themselves. And this "who" I'm discovering as a teacher is paradoxically yet fundamentally a student. Not formally, of course. I am now on the other side of the lectern. I prefer getting a paycheck to paying tuition. But my teaching reveals to me my essential character as a student in a much more basic way. I see how I am someone perpetually in need of an education. It does this best when I suspect this least.

This is part of the nature of a calling. A career consists of plans, but a calling is full of surprises. Success in a calling requires that you become less wedded to your expectations.

And while a career excludes, a calling includes. There is always a struggle between your career and your personal life; you inevitably cheat one or the other. But a calling abides in a balanced life. A sign of its success is when *everything* in your life is working.

From the outside, your calling may not look like much. But how it appears externally isn't really important. A calling isn't necessarily the top spot; it's your spot. It doesn't involve a hierarchy, at least in the sense of something that devalues all that lies below.

The ultimate difference between a calling and a career is this: With your calling, when you arrive, you like the destination. Thus, for your calling, anticipating your elder self becomes as important as remembering your younger self. Something that works as an ambition doesn't always satisfy as an achievement.

In the end, we rush because we are mortal. Our hurriedness is frustration with our limits.

Through our careers, we can try to deny this. If we make enough, we can turn time into a commodity. Money buys speedier technology. It brings others to do our bidding. But what we ultimately want isn't for sale.

So, we end up weary despite all our labor-saving devices. Stressed-out while surrounded by our toys. Running faster and falling further behind.

Peace begins rather with the discovering of a calling. This isn't a one-time event. It's a process that deepens. I've learned my hurried life doesn't come from others. At bottom, it isn't out there; it's in me.

Personal Reflection Prompts

1. Does your life ever feel *too* busy? That you're not getting to the things you want or need to accomplish? That the important stuff is always getting pushed aside, even when you wish it were otherwise? Stop for a moment and consider: Where does this busyness come from? When you do, what do you see?
2. Just as an experiment, try adopting a different angle of vision. Start by assuming you have *all* the time you need. Operating under this assumption, how do your overwhelming days or frantic moments appear now? Activist Ralph Nader once said, we live in a world in which whims become wants and wants become needs. How much of your day is filled with whims? with wants? Strip away from your planning everything except what you genuinely need to do today. What's left? And among what's left, what is most important?
3. How much of your busyness is out there and how much of it is in you? Feeling frantic or overwhelmed isn't always a matter of a particular situation or context. It can also arise because of something deeper within you. Take the opportunity to reflect upon your reactions to particular requests or demands in your daily activities. What is pushing your buttons? And even more importantly, why?
4. This essay introduces the notion of a calling in contrast to a career. In doing so, it echoes William Sullivan's discussion of callings in this chapter. Sullivan brings out the implications of thinking of our motivations as a "calling" rather than "drives." Seeing motivations as a calling fosters an outward orientation; conceiving of them as drives prompts an inward focus. How do you understand your motivations? If you were to reimagine them as a calling, how would it change the dynamics of your day?
5. Because of the way callings implicate a relationship to "something larger than yourself," they have an inherently spiritual character. A calling can be to

a personal role, say, becoming a mother. A professional role, such as envisioning a medical career. A more public role, inspiring you to speak up at a school board meeting. A calling can be as simple as planting a garden or as potentially impactful as saying hello to an elderly neighbor. What are the callings in your life? And what is the "something larger" they point to?

6. What can this "something larger" tell you about how you envision your purpose in your life?

***

Are you like me, always wondering about things? Did you ever annoy a parent, coach, or teacher by asking too many questions or doing so at inconvenient times? Or perhaps you've been a less-than-enthused recipient of someone else's unfiltered curiosity? If any of this is true, this essay is especially for you.

Wonder

Wondering about things can get you into trouble.

As a curious kid, I learned that early on, constantly annoying adults with questions and often encountering ones that were well beyond my grade school ken to comprehend. I remember distinctly around age 10, asking my parents, How do you know God exists?

I'd also drove some of my early math teachers up a wall, when I'd ask, "Why?" rather than simply memorizing the formulas they kept putting up on the board. I'm sure on more than one occasion, it made it hard for them to get through their intended lessons.

But it was a high school math teacher who came to my rescue. She must have seen something in me, something that at the time I couldn't articulate or understand, a philosophic bent I didn't yet know the words for. She told me to look up in the town library Pierre Teilhard de Chardin, a Jesuit priest who died the year before I was born, and read one of his books.

Randomly picking one of Teilhard de Chardin's books from the library shelf, I immediately discovered I was in over my head. But I clumsily kept reading, and when I came upon his description of the Omega Point – the final point toward which the universe is heading – I was hooked. I doubt I understood much of what the Jesuit priest had to say back then, much less agreed with it, but upon reading him, I was off and running.

I've been off and running ever since.

In graduate school, I was captivated by Plato. I adopted as a kind of mantra, the philosopher's line in the Theaetetus: "Wonder is the feeling of a philosopher, and philosophy begins in wonder."

Curiosity can lead to wonder, but it's different than wonder. Curiosity can be satisfied once you've answered the question that originally spawned it. But wonder never ends – it abides and is sustained by the question. Wonder, as it's developed in my life, is more than a simple intellectual pursuit. It's a basic comportment, a way of being.

If you were to ask me why I am this way, what purpose it serves, I wouldn't have an answer, at least a ready one. At a fundamental level, it's for me more akin to breathing than a deliberative choice. And just like regularly inhaling, it keeps me alive.

Wonder for me involves more than simply something I don't at the moment understand. It doesn't just entail something that I haven't yet been able to explain. Much more fundamentally, it points to something that's unexplainable. St. Augustine's idea comes to mind: If you can comprehend it, it's not God.

Thus, unsurprisingly, my strongest moments of wonder have a reverential character.

These moments of wonder arise when I stop and bracket my run-of-the-mill engagements. Putting aside the brushing of teeth, the finding of socks, the emptying of trash, and the getting of mail.

I hit the pause button, bracketing all the chatter in my head. Routines dissolve. I take an unencumbered look at the world. A veil falls away and I see more deeply into things.

It's an uncanny, unsettling feeling, in which your awareness shifts gears. Objectively, nothing has changed, yet you experience everything differently. As you refocus, your surroundings – however ordinary – have a luminous quality, as if you are seeing them for the first time. And in a way, you are.

Living wondrously is living life as a continuing hypothesis, testing things as you go. It creates, as paradoxical as it sounds, a grounded openness, a place in your life in which faith can grow. It is sturdier than orthodoxy.

I remember holding my newborn daughter wrapped in a hospital blanket. Looking at her in wonder, I promised, "You don't know me yet. But I'm your father. I want you to know you can always count on me. Always."

To be sure, wonder can engender doubt. It can cause you to ask the questions you may need to ask. But when experienced most deeply, it enables you to be surer of things than is otherwise possible. As I spoke to my newborn daughter, I knew this was a promise I would keep.

Personal Reflection Prompts

1. This essay states: "Curiosity can lead to wonder, but it's different than wonder." In your view, what is the relationship of curiosity and wonder? Is wonder fundamentally different from curiosity or simply an extension of curiosity? Can you experience wonder without curiosity or have curiosity without a sense of wonder? If you had to give up one or the other, which one would it be?

2. Wonder, the essay suggests, can foster questioning, yet also make you surer of things than would otherwise be possible. This sounds at least a bit paradoxical: How can this be? If this juxtaposition of questioning and certainty has at paradoxical air, what might it mean for how you understand spirituality in your life? Do your spiritual experiences make you more or less certain about things? Is it possible to be deeply spiritual without certainty about your beliefs?
3. People often express wonder in relating their spiritual experiences. Jane Goodall expresses wonder in perceiving the intricacies of ordinary leaves: "Never had I been so intensely aware of the shape, the color of the individual leaves, the varied patterns of the veins that made each one unique." Consider the moments of wonder in your life. With as much clarity and detail as you can muster, how would you describe them? In attempting your descriptions, do words ever fail you? If so, why would this happen? Have you ever on any occasion been frustrated by the inadequacy of words?
4. Is wonder a fleeting, impermanent experience or an abiding basic comportment of character? Is "living wondrously" possible? Desirable? Useful? Advisable?
5. Has an encounter with wonder ever changed you? How so? Have you ever tried to repeat the experience? Did it work? Even if the experience of wonder later faded, did it leave some permanent mark upon your choices or outlook?
6. To recall again William Sullivan's discussion of purpose, is the capacity to experience wonder a gift?

6

Conclusion – And Now What?

Telling Your Own Story

> *"We shall not cease from exploration*
> *And the end of all our exploring*
> *Will be to arrive where we started*
> *And know the place for the first time."*
>
> T.S. Eliot

Endings as Beginnings

Knowing for the First Time

I stressed in the book's introduction the importance of beginning wherever you are. In a sense that T.S. Eliot recognized, that beginning is also where you end up, but now with a crucial difference. You know the place for the first time.

The book's larger aim has been to deepen your awareness and understanding of your own thinking as you engaged in the process of ethical reflection. In this sense, it is an undertaking aimed at self-knowledge. The "place" you can hope to know is you.

So, pause for a moment and ask yourself: What do you know now that you didn't when you first opened *Seeking Your Better Self*? Are there aspects of yourself that have come into a clearer focus? Do you have any new perspectives upon the important relationships in your life? Did you find yourself rethinking any of your previous choices or actions? Did you resolve to do anything differently in the future? Were there any insights that you came to know "for the first time"?

Your Undertaking of an Ethical Journey

It has been a bit of a ride for you, I'm sure. If you did it fully and well, I suspect it had its starts and stops, detours and turnarounds aplenty, moments of frustration

---

Seeking your Better Self: Timely Virtues for a Turbulent World, First Edition. Jeffrey Nesteruk.
© 2026 John Wiley & Sons, Inc. All rights reserved, including rights for text and data mining and training of artificial intelligence technologies or similar technologies. Published 2026 by John Wiley & Sons, Inc.

along with hopefully points of clarity and some measure of insights. I hope you laughed at least once or twice.

I'm grateful for you staying with me this far. I've attempted to keep my promise to you – trying as I mentioned at the start – of giving you a hard time lovingly. I hope you still regard me as an amiable companion. I admire you for taking that first step on a journey which – like all the best ventures – you couldn't know from the start how it would end. All our serious choices – I can't help but think of my marriage vows here – are fundamentally acts of faith.

Wobbly Moments

Even though fundamentally acts of faith, our serious choices are done with a certain amount of fear or trepidation. They have their wobbly moments. And yet: Amid that uncertainty, a choice is inevitable.

You have to learn to greet the shakiness of life, those out-of-balance times, with an awareness of their potential.

The secret is: Your wobbly moments – when you feel lost or uncertain and are struggling to get your bearings – are your best moments. These are the moments when you're ready to learn something about yourself, when there's an opportunity to see things anew, when you're most susceptible to engaging life in a deeper, more fulfilling way. I want you to have more of them and learn how to use them well.

It can be that in the most turbulent of times we try to resist our wobbly moments. We seek an easy peace, rather than a deeper struggle. You can cling to the steadiness of the shore instead of navigating the choppy sea. But the sea is always there.

Ethical Reflection

But just as the sea is always there, so is the intellectual raft of ethical reflection. Without the waters sustaining it, even when turbulent, the raft would go nowhere. In this way, wobbly moments can begin to unsettle the stagnant portions of your life. That's why, if you can learn how to use them well, they are your best moments.

And the ethical reflections they spur are key to using them well.

For, at their best, ethical reflections exhibit an affirming power, providing a balm for a hectic life, a saving grace in turbulent times. For at its core, ethical reflection rests on a belief that things can be different and things can be better. And it is within our power to make it so.

Guiding Virtues

But just as wobbly moments spur ethical reflection, so ethical reflection requires the virtues. This is because reflection itself can also go awry. It can become compulsive thoughts or undue worry or even troublesome fantasies. That is the reason ethical reflection must be grounded in the virtues. It can keep the dynamics of your mind from going off the rails.

Life-affirming reflection needs to reside in a praiseworthy character. It is as much a matter of who you are as the cognitive skills you may possess. Misdirected human intelligence, like its artificial counterpart, is a scary thing. I've known a lot of smart people in my life. Smart people are not always noble or wise.

Discerning Purpose

In connecting the developing of the virtues to the discernment of your purpose, it's worth recalling that your discernment here rests on an evolving recognition of the relationship you are claiming to your world. By providing touchstones for this process of such recognition, the four virtues support and enable your discernment of purpose. They do so through the personal development they foster, encouraging a movement from yourself to other persons to the things in your world to your larger aspirations. At each step, your choices help to shape the contours and content of the relationship you are claiming.

So, wobbly moments spur ethical reflection and ethical reflection requires the development of the virtues that support and enable the discernment of purpose. This is the ethical journey for which the book offers structure and support. It is the arc of your undertaking of moral reflection and development.

Putting It All Together

Wobbly Moments/Ethical Reflection/Guiding Virtues/Discerning Purpose – These four themes comprise the narrative progression of the book. It is my story that I have endeavored to share.

Now I am inviting you to craft and develop your own story. The book's motif of posing questions, encouraging you to adopt an evaluative posture in your undertaking of moral reflection, provides a starting point.

Endings as Beginnings

My intention is for this book's ending to be your beginning. Your undertaking of ethical reflection has been something of a "trial run," the first attempt at a practice I hope you continue to develop and make at integral part of your life. Getting better at ethical reflection is just like developing the many other skills you doubtless have already achieved. You move from novice to competence to expert. As William Sullivan emphasizes: "Like other habits of mind, reflection is a skill that can be modeled, taught, and consciously developed through a process that resembles developing expertise in any field."

As any successful musician or athlete knows, the process never ends. Nor would we want it to do so. For learning of this kind is an integral part of living well.

The Power of Stories

Philosopher Jean-Paul Sartre wisely remarked: "[A] man is always a teller of tales, he lives surrounded by his stories and the stories of others, he sees everything that happens to him through them, and he tries to live his own life as if he were telling a story."

As such, storytelling is powerful, even when cast as popular entertainment. For instance, the popular 1998 television sitcom, *Will & Grace,* has been credited with fostering a greater acceptance of homosexuality among a wider range of groups.

But storytelling is more than popular entertainment to which we turn for pleasure and diversion. Consciously or not, we are always telling stories about ourselves. New York Times Columnist David Brooks writes: "I believe most of us tell a story about our lives and then come to live within that story."

Such stories have an elemental influence. Brooks continues: "You can't know who you are unless you know how to tell a coherent story about yourself. You can know what to do next only if you know what story you are part of."

In creating your story, you are explaining yourself to yourself – and you do need to do so before you can explain yourself to anyone else.

As author Frank Rose at Columbia University's Digital Storytelling Lab writes, "The first thing you need to know as a storyteller is: Who are you, and why are you telling this story? What is your purpose, and how will the story you're telling help further it?"

In identifying these priorities for a storyteller, Rose reflects the trajectory of your undertaking of ethical reflection and exploration. For your undertaking began with developing a coherent conception of self – asking "who are you" – and expanded to a deepening of your discernment, grappling with the question of "what is your purpose."

Thus, as you craft a story drawing from your undertaking of ethical reflection and exploration, Rose's account of storytelling prompts two further questions: First, "Why are you telling this story"? Second, "How will the story you're telling help further" your purpose?

The "why" for your story, your reason for crafting it, is to affirm and strengthen the transformative insights of your ethical reflection, integrating them into your life. "A good story," writes Rose, "is like a road. It takes you on a journey. Things happen along the way – conflicts rear, defeat looms, the battle is won or lost, a transformation occurs." In working to develop your story, you can solidify and deepen your transformation, moving decidedly from thoughts to action.

The "how" for your story, its help in furthering your purpose, lies in the larger transformation strong personal stories can engender. Rose adds that stories not only change the protagonist: "[T]he audience will be taken on a journey as well, starting in one state, emotionally or intellectually or imaginatively speaking, and ending in another." In solidifying and deepening your own transformation, you can foster the growth of others from "starting in one state" to "ending in another."

Owning Your Life

Stories have great power, but it is a power that lies largely dormant until you decide to tell – and live – your own story.

If you don't craft and develop your own story, you can never really own your life. You'll end up as a character in someone else's story. And someone who likely may not have your own interests at heart. That, at a minimum, is what the deeper reflection of *Seeking Your Better Self* is trying to overcome. More than we often realize, we are living according to a script we didn't write. It's the subtlest form of coercion. It does its work without us even knowing it's there.

Telling your story is what gives yourself – who you are – a stable and enduring quality. Coupled with this steady character, the narrative you embrace is also creative and actionable. This is because it is *your* story in two senses: It is yours because it bears your unique personal imprint and yours because it serves as the foundation for your future choices.

Telling Your Own Story

Stepping Out

So, wobbly moments spur ethical reflection and ethical reflection requires the development of the virtues that support and enable the discernment of purpose. This is the ethical journey for which the book offers structure and support. It is the arc of your undertaking of moral reflection and development.

It is now the source of the story you are ready to tell.

In engaging the readings, questions, and exercises in the book thus far, you have already begun to craft and develop your story. At least in inchoate form, a number of the pieces are already there. The next step – the step I'm asking you to take now – is to put it all together and to do so in a powerful way.

As you start out to craft your story, I've provided you with a model. As you'll see, the model consists of a schema that recalls the steps of ethical reflection and exploration that have marked your undertaking thus far. Drawing upon those steps of ethical reflection and exploration, I've elaborated a bit at points on this schema to be helpful. Your aim now in developing your story is to knit together the steps you've taken up to this point into a larger coherent narrative. How do you want the pieces of yourself to fit together?

In whatever manner you choose in creating your own story, you may draw upon your wobbly moments, the values that emerged from your ethical reflections as you grappled with those moments, the attributes of character – the virtues – you developed as you sought to embody those values, and the purpose your evolving character enabled you to discern. You may draw upon these elements in whatever manner you choose because the story you're now creating is *your* own story, the story of who you are and where you want to go.

The ways in which people tell the stories of their lives and then live within them are manifold and plentiful. I regularly hear them from my students. Indeed, hearing such stories is one of the joys of teaching. Listen carefully to those you encounter daily and you will hear them too. These stories express and embody the commitments that give individual lives their coherent structure and purpose.

I need only look around in my life at those I encounter to offer examples. There's the lawyer who quits rather than represent a client in a questionable scheme. There's the father who commits to an exercise plan so he stays healthy enough to support his kids. There's a highly qualified candidate for the local school board who loses the election rather than compromising his values. There's a friend who bravely and successfully survives a cancer diagnosis. There's a work colleague who keeps a confidence even at a personal risk. There's the guy who is always struggling to say less and listen more.

The model below is meant only as a prompt for your own reflections as you craft the story of the life you want to live. Imagine it as a helpful interlocutor open to an exchange of ideas. As with the best exchanges, approach it not mechanically, but creatively.

The points the model highlights aren't boxes to check, but rather thoughts to explore. You should feel free to linger over the points that most engage you and skip those that fail to inspire.

Each step – from wobbly moments to ethical reflection to developing virtues to discerning purposes – might potentially become a source of the commitments you wish to inform your story. And with each step, you can refer back to earlier portions of the book to elaborate on the model's schematic points.

The story you craft provides the basis for explaining your values and aspirations to others in a powerful way. As Jonathan Gottschall in his book *The Story Paradox* writes, "This is because stories are the single most potent way of influencing other minds. They're the best means human beings have yet found for swaying one another so hard that we may stay bent forever."

But it is more than that. Developing this larger coherence to your values and aspirations imbues them with a motivating meaning and purpose. They thus become a more potent catalyst for you living fully and well.

So, in crafting your story, you are defining your version of a good life and, likewise, providing the impetus to live it.

You start wherever at the moment you are. So, like my story's point of departure, your story begins with your own distinctive wobbly moments.

Step One – Wobbly Moments

Your story begins wherever you are.

If your life is anything like mine, wobbly moments regularly surface. They can be of a relatively routine sort:

> "My colleague isn't returning my text. Doesn't he realize how I need a timely response here? He's holding up the group project. But perhaps I wasn't clear? Could he have found something in my text off-putting? He hasn't been his usual productive self lately. Is there something more in his life going on? Should I check in with him? Would he welcome it? Or would he regard it as none of my business?"

They can also be of more lasting import:

> "Is it time to retire now? I'm pretty well off financially, but the stock market is crazy right now, so who knows? And I just read an article on the scary costs of long-term care should I become ill or incapacitated. But since I'm healthy at the moment, is now the time to do the travel I've always dreamed about? My spouse expects to work for a few years more. If she's working and I'm not, how will that change things around the house? And hey, this is new terrain for our relationship. Maybe I'll miss work more than I expected?"

In creating your story, consider your wobbly moments across four basic levels of your life. They could be wobbly moments that are now private, ones that you've never shared with anyone else. They could be moments of stress or uncertainty in your personal relationships or in the professional pressures at work. Or maybe there's a larger public dimension to your wobbly moments. Did you ever plan to give back to your college, religious group, or local community in ways you haven't yet followed through on? Doing the following four levels of inventory, you're likely to see that you might begin to tell your story in a number of ways. There is no need to feel compelled to give a priority to any particular approach. Remember to begin wherever you are, with the wobbly moments that are presently most meaningful or compelling to you.

Four Levels of Inventory

- Private Inventory
- Personal Inventory
- Professional Inventory
- Public Inventory

Step Two – Ethical Reflection

Your story can then emphasize the specific values of ethical reflection your distinctive wobbly moments call for as they unfold.

In this next step of ethical reflection, consider the key values that reoccur as you reflect upon and wrestle with your wobbly moments. In examining your values, call to mind the aspirations of clarity of thinking, deepening of emotion, expansion of perception, and affirmation of hope that contributed to the unfolding of your undertaking of moral reflection and exploration. As you look through the checklist below, what values have come to the fore as you grapple with your wobbly moments?

Integrity (clarity of thought)
- Consistency, Constancy, and Character
- Coherent Desire
- Coherent Thinking

Empathy (deepening of emotion)
- From the Familiar
- To the Far-off

Attentiveness (expansion of perception)
- Expanding Perception Outward
- Expanding Perception Inward
- Possessions, Practices, and Places
- Misfocused
- Unfocused

Openness (affirmation of hope)
- Stickiness
- Getting Unstuck
- You are never as stuck as it may first appear
- The world is always larger than it initially seems

Step Three – Guiding Virtues

Underlying the values of ethical reflection you are now drawing upon is the developing of the attributes of character – the virtues – that undergird and reinforce those values for the future.

Stories are not static statements or assertions. Movement constitutes their very essence. They start, develop, and then go forward. They have a beginning, a middle, and an ending.

Steps one and two are the beginning of the story you wish to tell about yourself. You might think of your wobbly moment as an opening scene, the friction or conflict that demands your thought or requires action. Your ethical reflection enables you to discern the important ethical values you wish to inform and guide your story.

But now what drives your story forward, what provides the substance for the middle of your narrative, is your character.

One of the most famous approaches for developing character comes from Benjamin Franklin. During his lifetime, Franklin devised a plan for "moral perfection," as he put it. It included an array of self-professed virtues, ranging from "temperance" to "frugality" to "sincerity," adding "humility" after being prompted by a Quaker friend taking note of Franklin's "pride." He aimed to develop one virtue at a time and kept a record in a notebook, noting infractions with a black mark each time one occurred. As Franklin freely admitted, he regularly fell short of his aspirations toward perfection.

I need look no further than my own life to believe Franklin's ready admission of a lack of perfection to be well-advised. Had I dared (even the thought prompts a shudder) to keep a notebook as he did, I suspect it would have had an ample amount of black marks.

Yet undeniably, there is something clear-sighted about his plan. He acknowledged the need for practice in developing his chosen virtues, aware that habits take time to form and evolve into character. He also wisely chose to focus on only a single virtue at a time, avoiding the overwhelming ideal of an immediate and full-fledged transformation. Via his notebook, he did a regular review and made personal reflection an essential part of the process.

In creating your own story, you might take a cue from Franklin. Certainly, the practice he adopted is likely to be the longer portion of your story, the substantial middle part as it moves forward. Just as Franklin approached the development of chosen virtues sequentially, you might prudently focus on the four virtues below – holistic mind, empathetic heart, attentive eye, open spirit – one at a time. As the saying goes, the perfect is often the enemy of the good. From Franklin, we can learn how to be morally kind to ourselves, clear-eyed toward our imperfections, yet embracing an ongoing commitment for improvement.

- *Holistic Mind*
- *Empathetic Heart*
- *Attentive Eye*
- *Open Spirit*

Step Four – Discerning Purpose

In connecting this developing character to the world now emerging, you can discover your purpose.

The strength of your story thus far will depend heavily on its coherence. It is in knitting together the prior three steps that your story will begin to shape its potency, its power that is capable of motivating you and persuading others.

But it is with your discernment of purpose that your story's potency comes to its full fruition. As we noted earlier, your purpose is what defines the connection of yourself to your world. In doing so, it reveals your aspirations, the goals you hope to bring to realization. In storytelling terms, it represents not the beginning or middle of your narrative, but the aspiring end of your story. As the hoped-for end of your story, your purpose necessarily informs the meaning of the earlier parts of your narrative.

As it defines the relationship between yourself and your world, your discerning of purpose doesn't occur in isolation, but is informed by your understanding of the reality of world in which you live. What does your world need now? Different circumstances call forth different purposes. So, in creating the end for your story, in choosing your aspirations, what does your world call for today?

Shakespeare's famous line of "All's well that ends well" may strike many of us today as merely poetic. But the recent research of psychologists Daniel Kahneman and Barbara Fredrickson reveals how the end of an experience disproportionately affects the way people remember the quality of the experience. Known as the Peak-End Rule, it suggests our recollections of an experience tend to focus on its powerful and concluding moments. All this suggests the purpose you incorporate into your story will have a preeminent effect on its power and influence.

So, as you consider the aspiring end of your story, reflect on these three essential steps discussed earlier in the book for discerning your purpose:

- *Recognizing Your Talents*
- *Reframing Them as Gifts*
- *Asking What Your World Needs*

And Now What?

A psychologist friend of mine tells me that many of his clients in their thirties or forties are, in one way or another, asking: And now what? I can certainly see how it would be a common question for those approaching or in midlife. At that point, you might well have accomplished some of your goals and likely discovered that some of them haven't fully lived up to your initial expectations. So, with much of your life likely still ahead, you're inclined to ponder: What next?

I think, though, it's a question that has a larger salience beyond those entering midlife transitions. I've seen it in students throughout their college years and then as graduation approaches and they confront new life choices. I've also seen this "And now what?" query arise in the minds of friends as they contemplate retirement. What comes after the careers they have thus far dedicated the bulk of their lives to?

Really, this is a question for anyone going through a transition and thus, significantly, is a reoccurring challenge for all of us. Indeed, as I said at the outset, struggling with my personal transitions was the underlying motivation for my writing of this book. As I write these final words, I have a personally satisfying sense of forward motion in my life. I hope that in reading this book, you have received some comforts or insights as you face the "and now what" in your own life. Thank you for joining me in this common undertaking.

It's an undertaking that reflects a perennial quest: How to be your better self? How to tap your ideals? How to define your version of a good life and then to live it? It's a reminder that living a simple decent life is a goal worthy of us all – and something we are all capable of.

As you create your own stories, I wish you well. Of course, this is only a beginning. But beginnings are no small matter.

Notes

1 For ease and engagement of the readers, I have used "ethics" and "morals" interchangeably throughout the text. In more technical contexts, distinctions are sometimes drawn between the two, such as viewing "ethics" as prescriptive and "morals" as descriptive.
2 I have also generally used "feelings" and "emotions" in a nontechnical fashion. Within a more technical framework, emotions may be characterized as automatic physiological responses and feelings as conscious interpretations of these experiences.

Bibliography

Aristotle (2009). *The Nicomachean Ethics* (W.D. Ross & L. Brown Trans.). Oxford University Press.

Bentham, J. (1970). *An Introduction to the Principles of Morals and Legislation*. In J.H. Burns & H.L.A. Hart (Eds.). Athlone Press.

Berry, W. (2002). *The Art of the Commonplace: Agrarian Essays of Wendell Berry*. In N. Wirzba (Ed.). Counterpoint.

Brickman, P. & Campbell, D.T. (1971). Hedonic relativism and planning the good society. In M.H. Appley (Ed.), *Adaptation Level Theory* (pp. 287–305). Academic Press.

Brooks, D. (2023, September 21). A theory of Elon Musk's maniacal drive. *The New York Times*. https://www.nytimes.com/2023/09/21/opinion/elon-musk-ambition.html

Carroll, L. (2023). *Alice in Wonderland*. In D.J. Gray, (Ed.), 4th ed. W.W. Norton & Company.

Clydesdale, T. (2015). *The Purposeful Graduate: Why Colleges Must Talk to Students About Vocation*. University of Chicago Press.

Descartes, R. (1983). *Principles of Philosophy* (V.R. Miller & R.P. Miller Trans.). D. Reidel Publishing Company.

Dewey, J. (1929). *The Quest for Certainty: A Study of the Relation of Knowledge and Action*. Putnam.

Duckworth, A.L., Gendler, T.S., & Gross, J.J. (2016). Situational strategies for self-control. *Perspectives on Psychological Science* 11(1), 35–55. https://doi.org/10.1177/1745691615623247.

Emerson, R.W. (1979). *The Collected Works of Ralph Waldo Emerson* (Vol. 2). Belknap Press.

Festinger, L. (1968). *A Theory of Cognitive Dissonance*. Stanford University Press.

Seeking your Better Self: Timely Virtues for a Turbulent World, First Edition. Jeffrey Nesteruk.
© 2026 John Wiley & Sons, Inc. All rights reserved, including rights for text and data mining and training of artificial intelligence technologies or similar technologies. Published 2026 by John Wiley & Sons, Inc.

Fredrickson, B.L. & Kahneman, D. (1993). Duration neglect in retrospective evaluations of affective episodes. *Journal of Personality and Social Psychology* 65(1), 45–55. https://doi.org/10.1037/0022-3514.65.1.45.

Frost, R. (n.d.) The death of the hired man. *Poetry Foundation*. poetryfoundation.org/poems/44261/the-death-of-the-hired-man (accessed on 2025, 12 December).

Gladwell, M. (2009). *Talking to Strangers: What We Should Know About the People We Don't Know*. Little, Brown and Company.

Goodpaster, K.E. (2007, October 22). *Teleopathy*. Sage Publications. sk.sagepub.com/ency/edvol/ethics/chpt/teleopathy.

Gottschall, J. (2021). *The Story Paradox: How Our Love of Storytelling Builds Societies Up and Tears Them Down*. Basic Books.

Haidt, J. (2005). *The Happiness Hypothesis: Finding Modern Truth in Ancient Wisdom*. Basic Books.

Haidt, J. (2013). The *Righteous Mind: Why Good People are Divided by Politics*. Vintage Books.

Haidt, J. (2024). *The Anxious Generation: How the Great Rewriting of Childhood is Causing an Epidemic of Mental Illness*. Penguin Random House.

Hartman, E. (1994). The commons and the moral organization. *Business Ethics Quarterly* 4(3), 253–269.

Higgins, R. (2024). *Thoreau's God*. The University of Chicago Press.

James, W. (2012). *The Varieties of Religious Experience*. In M. Bradley (Ed.). Oxford University Press.

Kahneman, D., Fredrickson, B.L., Schreiber, C.A. et al. (1993). When more pain is preferred to less. *Psychological Science* 4(6), 401–405. https://doi.org/10.1111/j.1467-9280.1993.tb00589.x.

Kant, I. (2002). *Groundwork for the Metaphysics of Morals* (A.W. Wood Trans.). Yale University Press.

Kierkegaard, S. (2005). *Fear and Trembling* (A. Hannay Trans.). Penguin.

Lanier, J. (2010). *You Are Not a Gadget: A Manifesto*. Alfred A. Knopf.

Lewis, C.S. (1961). *An Experiment in Criticism*. Cambridge University Press.

Lewis, C.S. (2021). *Mere Christianity*. Harper Collins.

Lin, P. (2024, September 6). Amara's law and its place in the future of tech. *IEEE Computer Society*. computer.org/publications/tech-news/trends/amaras-law-and-tech-future

McVeigh, B.J. (2002). *The Self-Healing Mind: Harnessing the Active Ingredients of Psychotherapy*. Oxford University Press.

Mollick, E. (2024). *Co-Intelligence: Living and Working with AI*. Penguin Random House.

Mooz, H., Forsberg, K., & Cotterman, H. (2003). *Communicating Project Management: The Integrated Vocabulary of Project Management and System Engineering*. Jossey-Bass.

Munson, R. (2025). *Ingenious: A Biography of Benjamin Franklin, Scientist.* W.W. Norton & Company.

Myers, D.G. (2022). *How Do We Know Ourselves? Curiosities and Marvels of the Human Mind.* Farrar, Straus and Giroux.

Nietzsche, F.W. (1974). *The Gay Science: With a Prelude in Rhymes and An Appendix* (W. Kaufman Trans.). Vintage Books.

Plato (2007). *The Republic* (D. Lee Trans.). Penguin Classics.

Putnam, R.D. (2000). *Bowling Alone: The Collapse and Revival of American Community.* Simon & Schuster.

Rawls, J. (1999). *A Theory of Justice* (Revised Edition). Belknap Press of Harvard University Press.

Rose, F. (2021). *The Sea We Swim In: How Stories Work in a Data-Driven World.* W.W. Norton & Company.

Sartre, J.P. (1964). *Nausea* (L. Alexander Trans.). New Directions Publishing Company.

Sartre, J.P. (1989). *No Exit and Three Other Plays* (Vintage International edition). Vintage International.

Schweitzer, A. (1935). The meaning of ideals in life. *The Silcoatian*, New Series No. 5, 781–786.

Seneca, L.A. (1925). *Ad Lucilium Epistulae Morales* (Vol. 2) (R.M. Gummere Trans.). William Heinemann, G.P. Putnam's Sons.

Slatalla, M. (2025, February 13). Now that I'm sober-curious, do I have to toss my beautiful bar cart. *Wall Street Journal.* wsj./com/style/design/now-that-im-sober-curious-do-i-have-to-toss-my-beautiful-barcart-C44ef21c?gaa_at=eafs&gaa_n=ASW

Solomon, R.C. (1994). The corporation as community: a reply to Ed Hartman. *Business Ethics Quarterly* 4(3), 271–285.

Sullivan, W.M. (2016). *Liberal Learning as a Quest for Purpose.* Oxford University Press.

Thaler, R.H. & Sunstein, R.C. (2008). *Nudge: Improving Decisions About Health, Wealth, and Happiness.* Yale University Press.

Thoreau, H.D. (1971). *Walden.* (J.L. Shanley Trans.). Princeton University Press.

Tolstoy, L. (2009). *The Death of Ivan Ilych* (I. Preiblatt Trans.). Melville House Publishing.

Twain, M. (2022). The Innocents Abroad. *Project Gutenberg.* Gutenberg.org/files/3176-h/3176-h.htm#CONCLUSION

United States Public Health Services, Office of Surgeon General (2023, May 3). *Our Epidemic of Loneliness and Isolation.* hhs.gov/sites/default/files/surgeon-general-social-connection

Uplift Kids (n.d.). *21 examples of spiritual experiences.* upliftkids.org/spiritual-experiences/ (accessed on 2025, 12 December).

Vidra, R. (2025, January 28). Teaching is harder now. *Inside Higher Ed.* insidehighered.com/opinions/views/2025/01/28/thoughts-20-years-college-teaching-opinion

Weiner, E. (2024). *Ben & Me: In Search of a Founder's Formula for a Long and Useful Life.* Avid Reader Press, Simon & Schuster.

Whitman, W. (2016). *Song of Myself with Complete Commentary.* University of Iowa Press.

Wittgenstein, L. (1981). *Tractatus Logico-Philosophicus* (C.K. Ogden Trans.). Routledge.

Wordsworth, W. (1950). *William Wordsworth: Selected Poetry* (1st Modern Library Edition). Random House.

Zweig, J. (2025, March 16–17). The last decision by the world's leading thinker on decisions. *Wall Street Journal 285*, C1–C2.

As you create, develop and enact your own story, you may well continue to use this book as an ongoing resource for living your ideals. Below is a helpful Review Heading Index designed to provide you with ready access to *Seeking Your Better Self*'s key topics, insights, and exercises.

Review Heading Index

Seeking Your Better Self: Timely Virtues for a Turbulent World

1. Chapter 1: Introduction
   - 1.1. Doing an Inward Turn: p. 1
     - 1.1.1. Wobbly Moments: p. 1
     - 1.1.2. The Story I Want to Tell: p. 2
     - 1.1.3. Ethics as Relationships: p. 3
     - 1.1.4. The Four Fundamental Relationships: p. 3
     - 1.1.5. Raising Your Moral Sights: p. 5
     - 1.1.6. Beginning Where You Are: p. 6
     - 1.1.7. Bringing Your Whole Self: p. 6
   - 1.2. Tapping the Life-Enhancing Power of Reflection: p. 7
     - 1.2.1. Our Out-of-Kilter Lives: p. 7
     - 1.2.2. Keeping Reflection at Bay: p. 8
     - 1.2.3. The Hard Work of Reflection: p. 9
   - 1.3. Starting with the Virtues: p. 10
     - 1.3.1. A Preview of the Four Virtues: p. 10
     - 1.3.2. Clarity of Thought: p. 11
     - 1.3.3. Deepening of Emotion: p. 12
     - 1.3.4. Expansion of Perception: p. 13
     - 1.3.5. Affirmation of Hope: p. 14
2. Chapter 2: Our Relationship with Ourselves
   A Holistic Mind
   - 2.1. Becoming Yourself: p. 16
     - 2.1.1. It's Complicated: p. 16
     - 2.1.2. First- and Second-Order Desires: p. 17
     - 2.1.3. Claiming Yourself: p. 18
       - 2.1.3.1. Systemized Self: p. 18
       - 2.1.3.2. Serialized Self: p. 19
       - 2.1.3.3. Dramatized Self: p. 19

Seeking your Better Self: Timely Virtues for a Turbulent World, First Edition. Jeffrey Nesteruk.
© 2026 John Wiley & Sons, Inc. All rights reserved, including rights for text and data mining and training of artificial intelligence technologies or similar technologies. Published 2026 by John Wiley & Sons, Inc.

- **2.2.** Your Ethical Self: p. 19
    - **2.2.1.** Dynamics in Play: p. 19
    - **2.2.2.** Achieving Your Ethical Self: p. 20
    - **2.2.3.** Developing Your Narrative Self: p. 20
- **2.3.** The Relationship of Your Desires to Your Own Happiness: p. 21
    - **2.3.1.** Your Pursuit of Happiness: p. 21
        - **2.3.1.1.** Happiness as Satisfying Your Desires: p. 22
        - **2.3.1.2.** Happiness as Having the Right Desires: p. 22
        - **2.3.1.3.** Happiness as Overcoming Your Desires: p. 23
        - **2.3.1.4.** But Can You Ever Truly Know Your Desires?: p. 24
    - **2.3.2.** Reflecting on Your Desires: p. 24
    - **2.3.3.** From Your Desires to Your Thoughts: p. 25
- **2.4.** The Relationships of Your Principles to Your Judgments: p. 26
    - **2.4.1.** Reflective Equilibrium: p. 26
    - **2.4.2.** Contradiction as the Stimulus for Personal Growth: p. 27
    - **2.4.3.** Some Exercises: p. 27
    - **2.4.4.** Tell the Truth: p. 28
    - **2.4.5.** Keep Your Promises and Treat Everyone Equally: p. 29
    - **2.4.6.** Personalizing Reflective Equilibrium: p. 29
- **2.5.** Topical Reflections: p. 30
    - **2.5.1.** Joy: p. 31
    - **2.5.2.** Stress: p. 33
    - **2.5.3.** Boredom: p. 36
    - **2.5.4.** Work: p. 38
    - **2.5.5.** Mistakes: p. 40
    - **2.5.6.** Weariness: p. 42
3. Chapter 3: Our Relationship with Others
   An Empathetic Heart
    - **3.1.** Discovering Your Social Self: p. 45
        - **3.1.1.** From Integrity to Empathy: p. 45
        - **3.1.2.** Evading the Ego Trap: p. 46
        - **3.1.3.** An Undercurrent of Loneliness: p. 46
        - **3.1.4.** Our Precarious Common World: p. 47
        - **3.1.5.** Transformational Communities: p. 48
    - **3.2.** Friendship: p. 49
        - **3.2.1.** Reflecting upon Friendship: p. 49
        - **3.2.2.** Three Types of Friendship: p. 50
            - **3.2.2.1.** Friendship Based on Pleasure: p. 50
            - **3.2.2.2.** Friendship Based on Utility: p. 51
            - **3.2.2.3.** Friendship Based on Virtue: p. 52
        - **3.2.3.** Working Toward an Empathetic Heart: p. 53

- **3.3.** Beyond Friendship: From the Familiar to the Far Off: p. 54
    - **3.3.1.** Extending Your Empathy: p. 54
    - **3.3.2.** A Dip into Ethical Theory: p. 54
    - **3.3.3.** An Example to Get You Started: p. 55
    - **3.3.4.** Three Ethical Theories: p. 56
        - **3.3.4.1.** Bentham on the Consequences of a Person's Actions: p. 57
        - **3.3.4.2.** Kant on a Person's Actions: p. 59
        - **3.3.4.3.** Aristotle on a Person's Character: p. 60
- **3.4.** Topical Reflections: p. 61
    - **3.4.1.** Friends: p. 62
    - **3.4.2.** Conversation: p. 64
    - **3.4.3.** Forgiveness: p. 66
    - **3.4.4.** Sacrifice: p. 68
    - **3.4.5.** Complaining: p. 71

4. Chapter 4: Our Relationship with Things
An Attentive Eye
- **4.1.** Developing Your Attentive Eye: p. 74
    - **4.1.1.** Unsimple Simplicity: p. 74
    - **4.1.2.** Expanding Your Perceptions Outward: p. 75
    - **4.1.3.** A Doing-Something-Different Challenge: p. 77
    - **4.1.4.** Expanding Your Perceptions Inward: p. 77
    - **4.1.5.** Using Your Imagination: p. 77
- **4.2.** Possessions, Practices, Places: p. 79
    - **4.2.1.** Nudges: p. 79
    - **4.2.2.** Possession and a Culture of More: p. 80
        - **4.2.2.1.** Quantitative Measurements and Qualitative Judgments: p. 80
        - **4.2.2.2.** Asking the Why Question: p. 81
        - **4.2.2.3.** Personalizing the "Why" Question: p. 81
        - **4.2.2.4.** You Have More Possessions than You Know: p. 82
    - **4.2.3.** Practices: p. 83
        - **4.2.3.1.** Taking in the Array of Practices: p. 83
        - **4.2.3.2.** Private Routines: p. 84
        - **4.2.3.3.** Group Rituals: p. 84
        - **4.2.3.4.** Social Practices: p. 85
    - **4.2.4.** Places: p. 85
        - **4.2.4.1.** Your Places of Insight: p. 87
    - **4.2.5.** Artificial Intelligence: p. 87
- **4.3.** The Moral Risks of Your Moral Tilts: p. 89
    - **4.3.1.** Discerning Moral Risks: p. 89
    - **4.3.2.** Misfocused: The Distortion of Attention: p. 89

- **4.3.3.** Teleopathy in Your Own Life?: p. 90
- **4.3.4.** Unfocused: The Distraction of Attention: p. 91
- **4.3.5.** Discerning Purpose: p. 91
- **4.3.6.** Recognizing Your Distractions: p. 92
- **4.4.** Topical Reflections: p. 92
    - **4.4.1.** Details: p. 92
    - **4.4.2.** Home: p. 95
    - **4.4.3.** Self-Image: p. 97
    - **4.4.4.** Artificial Intelligence: p. 99
5. Chapter 5: Our Relationship with That Which is Greater than Ourselves
An Open Spirit
    - **5.1.** Your Self-Transcending Nature: p. 102
        - **5.1.1.** Getting Unstuck: p. 102
        - **5.1.2.** From the Problems *in* Your Life to the Purpose *of* Your Life: p. 103
        - **5.1.3.** A Striking Quality of Consciousness: p. 104
        - **5.1.4.** Turning to Spirituality: p. 104
        - **5.1.5.** That Which is Greater than Ourselves: p. 105
        - **5.1.6.** Engaging Spirituality Together: p. 106
    - **5.2.** First-Person Spiritual Experiences: p. 106
        - **5.2.1.** Jane Goodall, Scientist: p. 107
        - **5.2.2.** Paul Simon, Singer/Songwriter: p. 107
        - **5.2.3.** Oprah Winfrey, TV Host: p. 107
        - **5.2.4.** Edgar Mitchell, Astronaut: p. 108
    - **5.3.** The Misguided Attempt for Clear and Distinct Ideas, or Why Descartes Was Wrong: p. 108
        - **5.3.1.** Knowing Ourselves as Subjects: p. 108
        - **5.3.2.** Living Our Lives as Objects: p. 108
        - **5.3.3.** Illusive Certainty: p. 108
    - **5.4.** Pointers, Intimations, and the Ineffable in Our Lives: p. 110
        - **5.4.1.** Articulating the Ineffable: p. 110
        - **5.4.2.** Poetic Language: p. 111
    - **5.5.** A Personal Peace that Surpasses My Understanding: p. 112
        - **5.5.1.** Wisdom for an Open Spirit: p. 114
        - **5.5.2.** Discerning Purpose: p. 114
        - **5.5.3.** Virtues as Gifts: p. 116
        - **5.5.4.** "Drives" and "Callings": p. 116
    - **5.6.** Topical Reflections: p. 117
        - **5.6.1.** Worship: p. 117
        - **5.6.2.** Sleep: p. 120
        - **5.6.3.** Thinking: p. 122
        - **5.6.4.** Interruptions: p. 124

- **5.6.5.** Time: p. 126
- **5.6.6.** Wonder: p. 129
6. Chapter 6: Conclusion – And Now What?
   - **6.1.** Endings as Beginnings: p. 132
     - **6.1.1.** Knowing for the First Time: p. 132
     - **6.1.2.** Your Undertaking as an Ethical Journey: p. 132
     - **6.1.3.** Wobbly Moments: p. 133
     - **6.1.4.** Ethical Reflection: p. 133
     - **6.1.5.** Guiding Virtues: p. 133
     - **6.1.6.** Discerning Purpose: p. 134
     - **6.1.7.** Putting It All Together: p. 134
     - **6.1.8.** Endings as Beginnings: p. 134
   - **6.2.** The Power of Stories: p. 135
     - **6.2.1.** Owning Your Life: p. 136
   - **6.3.** Telling Your Own Story: p. 136
     - **6.3.1.** Stepping Out: p. 136
     - **6.3.2.** Step One – Wobbly Moments: p. 138
     - **6.3.3.** Step Two – Ethical Reflection: p. 139
     - **6.3.4.** Step Three – Guiding Virtues: p. 139
     - **6.3.5.** Step Four – Discerning Purpose: p. 141
   - **6.4.** And Now What?: p. 141

Printed and bound by CPI Group (UK) Ltd, Croydon, CR0 4YY
09/04/2026

14858157-0001